Girls' Life

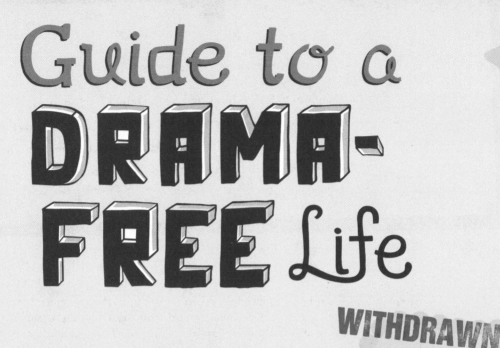

Guide to a DRAMA-FREE Life

From the creators of
Girls' Life magazine

Edited by Sarah Wassner Flynn

Scholastic Inc.

New York   Toronto   London   Auckland
Sydney   Mexico City   New Delhi   Hong Kong

Credits and acknowledgments:

Special shout out to Karen Bokram and the fab *Girls' Life* staff,
plus these awesome writers: Dawn Marie Barhyte, Jodi Bryson, Amanda Forr,
Jeannie Kim, Elisa Klein, Marissa Kristal, Lisa Mulcahy, Sandy Fertman Ryan,
Laura Sandler, Michelle Silver, and Erika Sorocco

ISBN 978-0-545-21493-3

Published by Scholastic Inc.
SCHOLASTIC and associated logos are trademarks and/or registered trademarks of Scholastic Inc.

12 11 10 9 8 7 6 5 4 3 2 1   10 11 12 13 14 15/0

Illustrated by Bill Thomas
Designed by Angela Jun and Two Red Shoes Design
Printed in the U.S.A.   40
First printing, September 2010

This book is for informational purposes only and not intended as medical advice and should not replace the advice of or treatment by any health-care professional. You should consult your doctor with questions about your physical and mental well-being. This book should be considered a supplemental resource only.

contents

*Introduction

So your BFF **isn't talking** to you because she thinks you spilled about her crush on the swim team captain (you *so* didn't). Your teacher just popped a 10-page paper on ya due the same day of your huge volleyball tourney. And then there's that guy that you've been head-over-heels in love with for years who's sending you all sorts of mixed signals. To top it all off, you can't find your fave cardi anywhere and, even though you swear your sis stole it, she's denying ever stepping foot in your room. *Ugh!*

Sound familiar? You're not alone. We've all got **drama** in our worlds—whether we want it or not. From your friends freaking out, to your sibs stealing your stuff, to your crush completely confusing ya, there's always someone—or something—that's gonna shake up your otherwise stable self. But before you crack, listen up. You *can* handle every dose of drama that heads your way. You just have to know the smart steps to do just that.

And that's why we're here. We've **talked to girls everywhere** to get their amazing insight on **how to deal with drama**—wherever it may come from. There's awesome advice and tips on figuring out the fellas, slaying school stress, getting along with the fam, and dealing with the rest of life's ups and downs. So start turning those pages, girl, and turn down the drama in your world!

The **best part** of this job has always been meeting with girls and hearing what is going on in their lives. **Often,** I am asked for some great life lesson or word of advice. I hardly know what to answer. We each go through such a **unique process** growing up, so how could I ever come up with one universal truth? But after giving it much thought, here goes: Never, ever leave frosted Pop-Tarts unattended in the toaster. Especially my toaster.

My toaster interprets the "light" setting as something just shy of a nuclear meltdown. I shudder to tell you about the morning I ran upstairs to blow-dry my hair, only to come back and find my breakfast flambé-ing nicely. While other breakfast foods, like toast and bagels, merely disintegrate into crumbs, you can apparently have a barbecue over a Pop-Tart.

I **panicked** at first and pulled the plug. Then I discovered the ancient Chinese secret of burnt Pop-Tart removal: chopsticks. Grab a pair, carefully grasp the offending Pop-Tart and, in one clean motion, fling it into the sink. So there you have it. *My one great truth*—a watched Pop-Tart never burns.

I know some people may **feel cheated** by this but, fact is, I have advice on a million things—and nothing at all. **Why?** Truthfully, as much advice as someone else can give girls, they often already have the best answers. Sometimes it takes hearing it from a **trusted person** (or their favorite magazine). Sometimes it takes talking over the problem. But most of the time, we girls just need someone else to say what that little voice in our heads and hearts is already telling us to do.

There is no crime in **asking for advice.** And there is even less crime in asking for help. Girls need to know that they are not alone in **this journey.** It's my hope that after reading this book, you will feel confident in dealing with the tough stuff. You just need to weigh your options, listen to people who genuinely care about you, and then, use your best judgment and do what you believe is right. So maybe that's **my best advice.** That, and get a toaster oven.

♡ KB

All About Your Buds

1

Friends—you can't live without 'em. They're the peanut butter to your jelly, the fries to your ketchup, the cherry to your hot fudge sundae, and, well . . . you get the picture. The truth is, buds really do make us complete. Whether keeping ya up all night with hilarious texts or being there with a box of tissues when you're bumming over a breakup, pals make us better—and happier—in so many ways.

But once in a while, friends can bring a whole lotta drama to your world, too. Especially if one talks behind your back, spills your secrets, or leaves you feeling left out.

Or maybe she's not so sneaky, but is supercompetitive with you over things like guys and grades, or continues to flake out on major plans. Whatever the sitch, there are a lot of issues that can send the two of you drifting apart like icebergs in Antarctica, and make you start questioning that "forever" part in BFF.

But not to fret: We've got the scoop you need to leap over any hurdle standing in your way when it comes to keeping your friendships fab. So, from making new buds to breaking up with the old, here's how to fix any friend prob—fast!

The Right Types of Friends

First things first: Do you have the right types of friends in your life? What does that mean, you ask? The right types of friends are girls who make you feel good about yourself. They should be interested in the things you do, *supportive*— and fun to be around, too. But not every friend will offer you all of these qualities, of course. Each one will contribute different traits to your crew, creating a rock-solid roundup of friends. Here are five gals you've gotta have in your world.

The Head Cheerleader

No pompoms or flirty skirt required. When you feel less than motivated, she's the go-to gal for a tender *lovin'* shove in the let's-get-it-done direction. Why? She has *loads of energy* and an infinitely sunny outlook on life. You're sure you don't have a shot at dunking a spot on the b-ball team? She doles out a dose of rah-rah that inspires you to give it your all.

The Study Buddy

She's not necessarily the smartest girl in your grade, but she's right up there in *conscientiousness.* You know, that trait that warms teachers up to you so they give ya bonus points just for the effort. This girl knows what's due when, and she'll save you *a seat in the library* if you want to join her for a study sesh. Big history project next term? You can count on this gal not to flake as your partner.

The Gossip Girl

Don't confuse the gossip guru for a rumormonger—that's not her game! She's never mean-spirited, and she refuses to pass on false info. In need of some *serious dish* or just have an itch to chat? Wanna know who got detention and why, or whom your *crush* is crushing on (you, please)? This girl has the juice on everything in and around school grounds. Drink it up.

How to Kick CLIQUES

Branch out! Get involved in different social circles, and focus instead on what makes you unique.

Don't judge! Your buds may be quick to jump on the new girl's geek-chic glasses, but you don't have to. Try to get to know her instead.

Speak up! Feel crummy when your pals talk about others? Be the one to change the subject. Or just leave the convo altogether. They'll get the hint.

The "Guidance Counselor"

It's hard to concentrate in class when something superheavy is crunching your brain. Maybe you had to bury your pet or you're having a major blowout with your BF after three-and-a-half weeks of bliss. Look to your no-nonsense pal to put it into perspective for you. She's rational, low-key, and keeps everything top secret. Best of all? Her advice is solid and you know she's looking out for you.

The Role Model

She's the yearbook editor a grade ahead of you—and you want her post when she moves on. Or it's that girl on your gymnastics team who always scores gold. She excels at what's important to you, so tune in to how she crops an image or sticks a dismount. Let her pave the way for you to join her up on the pedestal!

So maybe your friend *isn't so perfect.* She probably does that one thing all the time that drives you crazy (late, much?). But look at it on the *flipside:* You probably have your share of quirks that she puts up with, too. True friends learn to love everything about their buds, warts 'n' all. But that's not to say we should just accept these annoying habits. You'll be an even better friend by letting your girl realize (and fix!) her issues. *Score one for both of you!*

◎ She always arrives at least a half hour late.

Why don't you . . . help her get on the timely track? If your crew's meeting for dinner at 6:30, tell your girl to show by 6:15. Best-case scenario is she'll arrive *on time*—or even early—for once. But if she's still not there at 6:45, order without her. Once she realizes her friends won't be waiting around, she'll be more inclined to perfect her punctuality.

11

She's got her cell phone attached to her hand, and won't give it up—even for you.

Why don't you . . . lessen that obsession with texting and Facebooking by tipping her off? *Next time* her fingers start flyin', a simple joke like, "Hope there's not an emergency!" will give her a hint. Then, keep hang time special by suggesting everyone—including you!—*stash away cells* (though not too far, in case the 'rents call). When your girl sees that she didn't miss anything major during that hour she went phone-free, she'll stop thinking of it as a 24/7 accessory.

She butts into your—and everyone else's—convos.

Why don't you . . . give her confidence a kick? Most likely, your bud's a bit *unsure of herself* and inserting her unsolicited opinion makes her feel more important. One way to ix-nay her insecurity? Bring her into the loop before she forces her way in. The flattery you give your girl by asking for her thoughts on a subject will help her realize she doesn't need to commandeer every single conversation.

She is way boy-crazy. They're all she talks about!

Why don't you . . . remind her there's more to life than guys? While it's great to dish about *crushes* (what are gal-pals for?), obsessing over anything can be unhealthy. When she can't stop talking about sophomore Chad's power to capture her heart, redirect the convo toward something you know she'll be into, like her fave TV show. More to talk about means a *stronger bond*—and what could be better than that?

⊚ She always forgets her wallet, leaving you to pay.

Why don't you . . . slowly stop being her personal ATM? Your constant cash handouts may mean *she's taking advantage* of your generosity. Before you hang out, drop her a friendly reminder about having enough dough to cover the cost of the outing. And if you're sensing she doesn't have the funds? Have her over to your place for your mom's famous lasagna and a Wii marathon instead. *Totally free*—but just as fun.

⊚ She's a drama queen.

Why don't you . . . resolve to chat for *only fifteen minutes* the next time she seeks ya for one of her latest mini-crises? In that time, help her *focus on the positive* rather than rehashing the same stressful issues over and over. It's easy to get wrapped up in life's nonstop excitement, but don't let her latest drama eat up all your energy.

⊚ She tells it like it is—whether you want to hear it or not.

Why don't you . . . turn to her only when you need an honest opinion? *Choosing a first-date outfit?* Call her. Need an ego boost? Call, um, anybody but her. As long as you don't have unrealistic expectations, it'll be easier to appreciate how rock-solid and reliable she can be. Because after all, her brutal honesty can sting . . . but it can also save the day.

⊚ She's supercompetitive with you.

Why don't you . . . keep the competition friendly? Encourage each other to kick butt, but establish *a strict "no sore losers"* policy. No pouting, backstabbing, or begrudging. When she slips into showdown mode, make sure she knows there's room in the spotlight for more than one. And if she's totally harsh?

Have a *heart-to-heart* and explain that friendship isn't a contest. If she rivals you for something super-important, like your boyfriend, it's time to reconsider the friendship.

Toxic *Friends*

Sometimes *forgiving and forgetting* isn't so simple. Maybe your once-sweet bestie has turned beastly overnight. She's causing you to question your worth, or often leaves you feeling upset or bummed. If you have a bud who sucks the fun out of almost anything or just makes you feel icky, she is what we call a *toxic friend*—and she's someone who most likely doesn't belong in your life. *Here's how to figure out* if your girl's damaging your world, and what to do about it.

✦ She's a bad babe.

Friends who are *first to try* new things are often pretty exciting to be around. But it can get awkward and uncomfortable if your friend smokes, drinks, and hooks up with guys—as in, she's running laps on the fast track.

Should ya ditch her? It depends on whether she lets you do your own thing. As long as *she doesn't pressure* you to stray from your own values, it's fine to keep her as a friend. But let's say she asks you to cut class with her—and then gets mad when you won't. That's not OK. *Distance yourself* from friends who put you at risk for getting in trouble.

✦ She constantly cuts you down.

Friends should laugh with you, **give advice,** and keep crushes secret—not rag on you and make you feel bad. An occasional careless remark is normal, but what if she constantly belittles you?

Should ya ditch her? Decide if her comments are good-natured or *attempts to make her feel superior at your expense.* If she digs on you over sensitive topics or puts you down in front of others, that's not cool. Buds shouldn't embarrass you or stomp on your self-esteem.

✦ She uses you.

It's fun to **swap stuff** with friends and do each other favors. But some girls take advantage. It's hard to swallow, but sometimes it seems she's using you to copy your homework or bump up her wardrobe. Hey, where's that necklace she **"borrowed"** weeks ago?

Should ya ditch her? Be sure she considers your friendship **a two-way street.** Ask for a hand with a chore or to borrow a shirt. If she's true-blue, she'll help you out. If, on the other hand, she's only around when she needs something, her selfishness is over the top. *Friendship is about giving,* not just taking.

✦ She bosses you around.

Friends who take the lead and plan fun stuff are great. But if she tells you what to wear, who to befriend, and which clubs to join, **there could be a prob.**

Should ya ditch her? Ask yourself if your friend gives you room to be you. It's **OK** for her to be the activity director—as long as she also considers your wishes. A "my way or the highway" 'tude is rude. **Say you quit** soccer for violin, and she refuses to come to your recital. Friends should be a source of *support, not stress.*

✦ She's a backstabber.

It's one thing if she "**accidentally**" spills who you're crushin' on to your crew—then apologizes profusely for it. But if your **BFF** does something downright cruel or catty with little remorse, you have to question whether she ever was a "friend" in the first place.

Should ya ditch her? This one's pretty obvious: A BFF doesn't gossip about, or lie to, you. She doesn't share your *secrets* on her Facebook page. And a BFF definitely doesn't flirt with her best friend's boyfriend. If she does any of the above, it's time to *call it quits.*

GRRRR! It's a Friend Fight

So maybe your friend did something to really *tick you off.* Or maybe she's inexplicably angry about something you did. Now you're in a fight. *Ugh!* Fighting with your friends is one of the most uncomfy and awkward situations to be in. Even though conflicts stink, they're totally inevitable. Here's how to duke it out fair and square.

☺ Cool down

Getting *super-steamed* can lead to shouting or saying things you'll later regret. So before you reach the boiling point, call a time-out. *Walk it off,* write in a journal . . . whatever calms you down (and definitely keep your hands off the keyboard; IMing or texting always leads to statements you'd *never* make in person). Often, just taking time to *cool* can help a conflict blow over. You and a bud could realize you only fought because you were both in foul moods.

◎ *Resist the urge to get even*

While the idea of *getting back at someone* might feel good at first, doing something with malicious intent won't fix what started the fight in the first place. In fact, it will probably spur an endless, all-out, back-and-forth, get-back-at-each-other battle.

◎ *Pick the right time to talk*

Instead of confronting your bud before class about those rumors she spread, *ask to chat* with her after school, when neither of you is rushed or distracted. Can't find the right time to talk? Start off with an e-mail explaining your side. Hopefully, she'll reply with the same, and you can work things out online.

◎ *Speak up for yourself*

At times, it might seem easier to just let things slide but, if you make that a pattern, you're *denying* your own feelings—not a good thing. To make speaking out work for you, start by telling the other person specifically what she did to upset you. Instead of telling your girl, *"You're such a liar,"* try, "It bothers me when you tell me one thing and then totally do another." Tell her why you feel that way ("When you lie to me, it makes me feel disrespected."), and then *explain* what you'd like her to do differently ("If you just tell me the truth, I'll be okay with it.").

19

◎ Be prepared to apologize or compromise

First off, if you did something to upset or hurt someone (even if it was unintentional), *apologize*—and mean it. Then, see if you can find some middle ground—a compromise. Are you and your friend fighting because *you didn't tell* her about the crew's plans to hit the mall, even though you knew she was busy and couldn't make it anyway? Agree to include each other in plans, no matter what. Even if you *don't totally* agree with the compromise, you'll show respect for your bud and will hopefully be able to move on.

◎ Call a truce

Had about enough of this fight? Rather than going round after round, *call a truce.* If you still feel upset, try not to stew. Grudges only drag you down and keep you from getting on more positive footing. It's not the end of the world if everything doesn't work out to your expectations. Just be proud knowing you stood up for your feelings and did your best to *resolve the conflict.* Then go hang up those boxing gloves.

When Friendships Fizzle

If you and your pal just can't get past your differences, then maybe it's time to break things off once and for all. But before ya do, look into whether it's worth it to fix your floundering friendship. Here's how to figure out if it's time to say *adios* for good—or if you can buddy up again big-time.

What's New?

Since you've both outgrown dolls, it's time to find new common interests over which to bud-bond. Find activities both you and your friend can agree on. Try kicking it together at a martial arts class. Or, better yet, train for a charity run. There's nothing like sharing a passion for a good cause.

21

Blast to the Past

Relationships take ongoing effort. Fact is, it's common to hit rough patches with a friend as you mature, even if things always seemed easy before. **You're both growing and changing,** which can complicate matters. What to do? Remind yourself of what made you such good friends to begin with. Reminisce by collaborating on a special art project: Get some poster board, a little glue, and snapshots of you and your friend so you can make photo collages. One for you, one for her.

Close Encounters

Ignoring problems rarely makes them go away. Instead, refuse to accept the fault lines in a friendship until you've done all you can to repair them. Rather than toughing it out through those bouts of awkward silence, speak up. Be brave enough to say, "Hey, let's talk about how we can fix this." *Have an honest chat* about what's wrong, then put your heads together to figure out ways to make it right.

Be a Space Cadet

Spending every minute with your girl is unnecessary and not particularly healthy. *Give each other some space,* and don't veg out in front of the TV day in and day out.

● Spread Out

Friends aren't one-size-fits-all, so it's great to have a variety of pals. If you get to know different girls in your circle, you *won't sweat it so much* when your BFF seems off-ish. Make the most of the times she seems distant by building and strengthening your other friendships. Even if she's still your best friend, that doesn't mean she's your *only* friend.

MOVING ON

Have you decided that you've definitely outgrown the relationship? Well, there are right and wrong ways—and reasons—to end a friendship. Here's a step-by-step guide to breaking up with a bud.

Step 1 *Figure out what's wrong.*

What, specifically, bugs you about your friend? Is her behavior malicious or just annoying (there's a huge diff between spreading lies and, say, snoring at sleepovers)? Does your friend have wonderful qualities to balance the bad ones? Have you told her what is bothering you and asked her to change?

Pros	Cons
Smart	Bad Temper
Funny	Gossip

Before tossing a relationship, it's often worth trying to set things straight. And even if you ultimately decide the friendship can't be salvaged, you will have clearly thought through the situation. This will make the next step that much easier. . . .

Step 2 Say sayonara.

It's time to part ways? Offer a short and simple explanation, and then state that you want to end the friendship: "I've asked you to stop saying mean things to me. It makes me feel terrible. I'm sorry, but I don't want to be friends anymore." **Be clear and calm,** and don't verbally attack, which could cause things to spiral out of control and leave you feeling even worse.

Step 3 Expect the worst.

Even if you say your piece kindly and rationally, do not expect your friend to take it well. Nobody likes rejection, and your friend is no different. She'll likely defend her actions. If deep down you think she might have a valid point (maybe you did jump to a wrong conclusion or misjudge her), you might say, **"Let me think about it,** and let's talk again tomorrow when we've calmed down."

You might decide your friend deserves another chance after all, and maybe this is the wake-up call she needs to turn things

around. You're allowed to change your mind . . . or stick with your original plan. But in the end, you have to do what you feel is best for you.

Step 4 Allow yourself to grieve.

If you do end the friendship, you might feel a ton of emotions after your talk. Many girls feel a mixture of relief and also guilt, sadness, or anxiety. **This is normal.** It shows you're a caring person who doesn't like hurting others. And even though she wasn't an ideal bud, you might even miss the good parts of her.

So allow time to mourn the loss of this relationship. Talk to a parent or other buds about it—without badmouthing your ex-friend. **And give yourself a big pat on the back.** It's not easy to get rid of toxic buds, but know that you did what's best for No. 1—you!

When you have to DUMP YOUR BFF

REAL GIRLS WEIGH IN.

"My friend started hanging with the wrong crowd—a crowd that's super-mean. She always acted nice when she was around me, but I found out she was talking behind my back. So I told her we should stay away from each other."

—*Marianna*

"I put all the work into my friendship with my BFF. If I didn't plan a trip to the mall and the movies or find something fun for us to do, we did nothing."

—*Madeleine*

"My BFF always wanted to be partners in everything and never wanted me to hang out with anyone else. I didn't want to break her heart because she didn't have very many friends. So I just kind of avoided her. I said 'hi' when I saw her and no more. If you want to break a friend off, think about how many friends she has or how she will take it."

—*Laura*

Meeting New Friends

Whether it's because you've let go of that bad-news bud, moved to a new town, or simply want to expand your social circle, scoring some new friends can seem like a tough task. But believe us, getting some new crew really isn't that hard. Put this pal-making plan into action, pronto.

Be a bold babe.

Many girls think they have no control over whether people are going to like them or not. So they hold back, get shy, and wait to be approached. The smarter strategy? Be gutsy by making the first move toward potential buds. Smile and say "hi" to friendly kids you pass in the hall. Crank up

a convo with the girl who sits behind you in homeroom by complimenting her bag. Give your new lab partner props for figuring out that experiment. People dig people who are genuine and positive so just be your normal happy self. As for those random girls who don't respond to your outgoing ways? No loss. You want to hang with people who appreciate your cool, kind confidence.

Ask advice to break the ice.

An easy way to get to know someone? Ask for help. People love to be experts and like sharing what they know with someone who's interested. And, no, *asking questions won't make you look weird, dumb, or ditzy.* Inquisitiveness is actually a sign of curiosity and smarts. Say you're required to take a home ec class at school, but you have never sewed so much as a single stitch. You can't help but admire Emma's skills at hemming those jeans. So seek out her help. Try, "You're really talented at this stuff and I have no clue what I'm doing. Would you mind giving me a few tips?" Emma will most likely be more than happy to lend you a helping hand, and you'll get the chance to know her better.

Shake up your scene.

Stroll out of your comfort zone. You'll never meet anyone new if you're hangin' at the same places and doing the same stuff. Vary your routine. Sit in a different seat on the bus, walk a new way to school, take another hallway to your next class, sign up for an activity you've never tried. The plan is to put yourself in front of as many people as possible. Even if you don't say a word, they'll begin to recognize your face. Keep smiling, be sure your body language is friendly (no staring at the floor), and, soon, people will say "hey" to you. Take it from there.

Smart chat is where it's at.

When you're getting to know a fab new friend, listening is more important than talking. *Sure, this can be hard for some girls.* You could be gabbing your brains out about gym class, your icky little sis, and what happened last night on your fave TV show. But pay attention to what she's saying. If she sees that her thoughts matter to you, she's going to feel really good about buddying up in a solid way.

Is this new crew right for you?

Not to oversimplify things, but making new friends always comes down to basic respect—for the kids you're getting to know and for yourself. Only hang with a new gang if you feel they're putting forth the effort to totally appreciate your interests, ideas, and opinions as much as you appreciate theirs. Since you're going to be surrounded by so many new friends, you want to make sure they aren't the type to pull you down. *The right buds won't treat you any way other than terrific.* Because you deserve it!

Your BIGGEST Bud Dramas— SOLVED!

"My friend is very popular with the boys, so I am bombarded with questions from guys about who she likes. She's nice and deserves it—but I feel left out."

It's great that guys appreciate your bud's fabulousness like you do. But it can be annoying to field questions about her romantic interests. It's natural to feel a bit jealous of all the attention she gets. Yes, she probably deserves it, but you do, too. What you don't want is to let your feelings get in the way of your friendship. When guys come to you for the deets on your friend, politely but clearly tell them that if they want her number or whatever, they should talk to her. You're her friend, not her publicist. Hopefully, the guys will get the message.

"My BFF is going through a lot with her family. She's been really down and never wants to hang out anymore. She says, 'Maybe it'd be better if I weren't even here.' It freaks me out, and I'm scared. What should I do?"

You can't fix her family's sitch, but what you *can* do is be there for her. Withdrawal, depression, and suicidal comments are signs that she needs professional help. Urge her to talk to a teacher, counselor, doctor, or other trusted adult. Offer to go with her if it'd make her feel better. If she disses the suggestion, tell a trusted adult what she said. In this case, telling someone isn't being disloyal to your friend—it's sometimes necessary to break confidence to ensure a friend's well-being. Meanwhile, show her you care by letting her talk when she needs to, suggesting fun activities to do together, and reminding her you value your friendship.

P.S. Anyone in need of immediate help with feelings of depression or suicide can call the **Covenant House Nineline at 1-800-999-9999.** This call is free, anonymous, and won't appear on your phone bill.

"My BFF and I hang in different groups. Whenever I make plans with my friends, she asks why I don't want to hang out with her. She's not the problem—it's the girls she hangs out with. What should I tell her?"

Explain to your BFF that you love spending time with her but having your own group of friends is important to you. Not spending every moment together shouldn't damage your relationship. In fact, it could strengthen it. By planning quality, one-on-one time, you two are likely to really appreciate and enjoy each other's company rather than wasting time over silly stuff. If being BFFs and sticking to your own circles works for you two, fab! Otherwise, is there room for compromise? Do you like any of her friends? How about inviting her to hang with your crew this weekend? Worth a go, don't you think?

"Two of my buds always fight and want me to choose sides. When I tell them to work it out on their own, they get mad and tell me, 'If you were really my friend, you'd take my side.' They're both great friends, and I don't want to lose either of them. Help!"

Ugh. Friendship triangles can be complicated. And if you were to get involved in their spats, it would only further complicate things. No matter what, keep refusing to take sides. Let them know you are friends with both of them and do not want to get involved in their tiffs. Tell them it's unfair to put you in that position and that you would really appreciate it if they would understand that. If they keep pressuring you, declare in a joking but firm manner that you are Switzerland—you're the neutral party and won't choose sides!

THE BOTTOM LINE . . .

Hopefully, you'll figure out a way to make new friends and keep the old. But if you absolutely must break ties with a BFF, be diplomatic, especially if she's done nothing to hurt you. On the other hand, don't feel guilty about letting go of people who aren't good for you. That's part of growing up. When you boot a bad bud out of your life, you make room for an awesome new friend worthy of your coolness.

Figuring Out the Guys

Got boys on the brain? You're not alone. This is the time of our lives when fellas take front and center in our worlds. Whether you're starting to date or just thinking about it, boys can baffle you. *Does he like me? Am I his type? Am I sending him the right signals?* All of these questions and mixed signals can leave you feeling completely confused.

Don't ya wish you could just get inside of their minds once in a while? You know, to get a feel for what they're really thinking—and finally figure out why they do what they do. Well, while it's not possible to park yourself in their heads, we've got something *almost* as good: tried 'n' true advice about your cute counterparts, based on the experience of girls who've dealt with guys before ya. So don't let those dudes bring any more drama in your world—handle them with smarts and these savvy tricks.

CRUSHING 101

You can hardly concentrate in math, since he's only a row away. And when he passes you in the hall, your stomach does crazy flip-flops. Sigh! *Ah* . . . your first crush.

If it hasn't happened to you yet, believe us, it will. There will be a guy out there who is gonna occupy your every thought and send your heart racing, your head spinning, and your face flushing every time he comes within, like, 100 feet of you. Guys—especially the really adorable ones!—have a way of leaving us tongue-tied and taking over every other thought in our busy brains.

So, how to get your crush to, well, crush on you back? For one, it's important to note that some crushes, like celebs or your older bro's bandmate, are unattainable and best admired from afar (let's face it, dating an 18-year-old when you're 14 is totally out of the question).

But the more gettable guys—the captain of the cross-country team, your bio lab partner—are yours for the taking. Don't think your crush even knows you exist?

Just follow these tips!

✳ Make the First Move

It may not be the "traditional" thing to do, but guys definitely dig when girls make the first move. Believe us, it's better than their clumsy attempts to break the ice with goofy lines and other ways they try to impress you. So by approaching a guy with a simple, "What's up?" or "Did you download that new iPhone app?" you'll save him the stress of coming up with a cheesy opener.

✳ Get Sporty

Want an insta-way to wow a guy? Stock up on your sports knowledge. This isn't to say you need to know every single professional team in existence. You also don't have to pretend to be into it more than you are. But if the guy you're interested in happens to be wearing a Yankees hat, it'd be wise to know he's cheering for a MLB team. And

take advantage of any chance to get in on the game, be it going one-on-one on the b-ball court or challenging him to a soccer duel. Don't have the sporty skills? Don't worry—it's not about winning. The good thing about getting your game on together is that the two of you will have tons to chat about should other topics dry up.

✳ Charm Him

Sure, a cute dress may snag his attention. But what you're wearing will only get a guy initially interested—it's your personality that'll eventually have him hanging on for the long haul. Honestly. If you're at a party, don't huddle in the corner with your buds—put yourself out there in the middle of things and let the guys know you're in the room. Laugh at their jokes, tell some of your own. Whatever you can do to show off your sparkling personality will eventually captivate your crush.

✳ Listen Up

Flirting is to dating what the SAT is to getting into college: just another step in the process of getting where you wanna go. That means details definitely matter. Yes, you may be getting lost in a boy's baby blues, but they like when you pay attention to what he has to say. So listen to us, then seal the deal after a positive flirting experience by following up on something you learned during the convo. If he mentioned a big test or tryouts, send a text or Facebook message wishing him luck. After all, a little ego boost never hurt anyone, right?

Of course, relationships aren't one-way streets, so check that the guy is paying as much attention to you as you are to him. *If that's not the case, your attention is probably best focused elsewhere.* That's not to say you should give up entirely if a guy doesn't go for these moves right away. Just relax, be yourself, and hope for the best. With any luck, the guy you're chatting with will do the same.

"My brother's best friend has a crush on me. Every time he comes over, he tries to sit by me or flirt with me. I like him, just not in that way."

GL SAYS . . .

Subtlety can be the best bet to avoid hurt feelings, but it doesn't always get the message across. First off, don't flirt back. Drop hints, like talking about how great it is that you can be friends (key word) with your bro's buds. If he doesn't get it? Be more direct or ask your brother to nicely clue him in. Tell him you like him as a friend, nothing more. If you're worried about how he'll take it, tell him you have a rule against dating your brother's friends.

IS HE INTO YOU?

Now that you've got the guy's attention, it's time to figure out his feelings for ya. So let's say he chats you up in homeroom and walked home with you—twice! But he hasn't asked you to catch a flick or to go to the dance on Friday. Have your intuitions totally failed you? What's up? Here are some clues for what a guy will do if he's into you. . . .

❋ CLUE #1: He'll ask you out.

Simply put, if the dude you dig truly digs you back, he'll ask you out. It doesn't matter how slammed he is. Sure, no boy wants to stick his neck out only to get shot down. *But here's the thing: If he likes you, the possibility you'll say "yes" should be worth the risk.* He wouldn't want a braver guy to ask you out first. Right? So if weeks are flyin' by and your crush isn't suggesting any get-togethers, maybe he's not grooving on you. And that's not the end of the world. Really. It's his loss. You deserve a guy who recognizes how fab you are.

❋ CLUE #2: He's totally unattached.

Your crush flirts with you big-time on the bus every day. He's gonna be your BF—as soon as he breaks up with that girl who sits behind you in English. Which he says he's going to do . . . really, really soon.

Let's review: He strings you along while downright dissing his girlfriend behind her back. Way untrustworthy! If you were unfortunate enough to nab him as a BF, you can be sure he'd try to get cozy with other chicks on the sly like he did with you. A really great guy doesn't play two girls at the same time. *He'll be into you and only you.* So look for a crush who respects girls in general—and you in particular.

✿ CLUE #3: He's available.

You hung out with your crush last week and had the best time. He said he'd like to see you again, but now, when you see him at school, he cruises before you can even say "hi." What's up with that?

This is disappointing, no doubt. But don't beat your brain looking for that thing you must have done or said to repel him. You did nothing wrong at all. Even though it's ice-cold, some boys drop awesome chicks with no explanation. Maybe your cool confidence intimidates him. Maybe his 'rents don't want him to have a GF yet. Who knows—and it doesn't really matter. Just hold your gorgeous head high and move on.

CLUE #4: He pays attention.

When you told the world's worst joke, your crush was the only one who laughed. *When you mentioned you have mad candy cravings, sure enough, he slipped a bag in your desk.* He even asked how you did on the quiz that had you super-nervous.

No mystery here: This honey totally has the hots for you. When a guy is into you, he cares about the stuff that makes you tick. *Your next move?* Meet him halfway by asking about his favorite stuff. Let him know how impressed you were by that free throw he scored at yesterday's game. Take interest when he shows you the (ew!) bug collection he's been working on for two years. Whatever it takes, show some interest back, and you two will be totally vibing in no time.

ASK HIM OUT!

So you're pretty sure your dude's digging on you—but he hasn't asked ya out yet? What are you waiting for? It's totally cool for a girl to make the first move (of course, you already know that). Actually doin' it, though, can be tricky. You just need to know the no-fail "how can he resist?" secrets for totally capturing his interest—and getting that date!

Have It Your Way

The biggest mistake most girls make is planning the potential date around him. He tells a friend he had a great time bowling with his fam Friday so, even though you're so not an alley cat, you invite him to knock over some pins. Sushi makes you gag, but he loves it, so darn it, you're gonna suck it up and scarf that rainbow roll. Arrgghh.

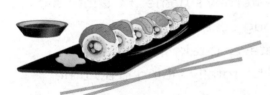

Why are you selling yourself short? Plan an activity you like, first and foremost. This is crucial, because when you're doing something that really gets you jazzed, the best parts of you show through— your enthusiasm, your sense of adventure, your fun side. This doesn't mean you should never take his interests to heart—it would be silly to plan a date he'd hate. Chances are he'll totally dig your confident, daredevil vibe.

●　●　●　●　●　●

What's His Sign?

OK, time to seize the opportunity. Your crush is alone at the bus stop, and he waves when he sees you coming. You head over to chat him up, but the sec you open your mouth, you involuntarily bust out a goony, honking giggle.

Get your game back by striking up some solid small talk—congratulating him on making the winning soccer goal on Saturday is a great place to start. While you're calmly chitchatting, look for subtle signs that your guy is into you. Does he stand a little bit closer than he needs to? *Does he rake his hands through his hair* once or twice (a classic diggin'-on-

Once you've thrown the big question out there, brace yourself for whatever answer he might toss back. Yeah, he could say, "No way," so be prepared for the possibility of a letdown. If he does decline, it's crucial not to crack. Keep your composure, smile at him, and just say, "OK, that's cool." Then walk away.

a-girl move that dudes do mindlessly)? Does he look you in the eye when you talk to him, but glance down and smile a lot when he talks to you? If so, jackpot city—his green light's sayin' go, but he's trying super-hard not to be glaringly obvious.

● ● ● ● ● ●

Poppin' the Question

So how do you know when to work the convo around to the point where you ask your guy out? Let a lull form in the conversation for a sec, then . . . just ask!

Do not ask him to explain himself. It doesn't matter if he likes another girl or is too intimidated to be seen on the dating scene or doesn't like the way you part your hair. These are his issues, not yours. You're a great gal with tons to offer—and a guy passing up the chance of a lifetime to hang out with you can't even begin to touch that. So if he says "Sure thing!"? Resist the urge to jump up and down like you just won a game-show prize. All that's left to do now is go out and have a blast!

43

WHAT ABOUT GUY FRIENDS?

Guy friends: gotta love 'em From the sporty dude who's always down for a game of one-on-one to the laid-back boy you can count on as a dance date in a pinch, each one adds his own special spice to your crew. But sometimes, it's hard to be "just friends" with a fella. A lot of girls end up falling in love with their BGFs.

And if that happens? It can work out—some of the best love stories stem from those who were friends first! You just have to be careful before you move into "more than buds" territory. Here's how to find out now if your connection is cool.

Get to know before it's a go Remember: Patience is a virtue. If you haven't been friends for very long, you should make an effort to get to know him even better before you turn him into your BF. Sure, he's cute when you're passing notes in class, but what if he happens to have a nasty habit of burping the ABCs? All of a sudden, he's not so Prince Charming.

The Real Reveal

If you want to get closer with your BGF, honesty is important. Sure, you've always been able to talk to him, but maybe not on a way-deep level. Well, this might be the time to let him in on that secret you haven't shared with anyone—like how you're nearly failing math. How he reacts will tell a lot. A guy who wants to deepen the bond may stun you by revealing an extra-deep secret right back. Or . . . maybe he'll clam up. And, yep, this could mean he's fine with being pals only. Don't be hurt or mad. You know where you stand, and you haven't done anything bold or awkward to trip up the friendship. No harm, no foul.

Friends are forever, fellas aren't

Don't force the issue. If you two are meant to be, you'll end up a couple eventually. But it's best to go slow for now. Boyfriends come and go, but real friends (even if they're guys!) will last a lifetime.

GL girls spill their DATING SECRETS!

What's your perfect first-date hot spot?

28%   The homecoming dance
27%   Go-karting, full-speed ahead!
25%   Home with pizza and a movie
11%   Sushi for two at a romantic restaurant
9%   A concert

It's date night and time for the check . . .

35%   Halfsies all the way, all the time
32%   Whoever does the askin' should pay
30%   The guy, of course
3%   Girls should step up . . . and foot the bill

Would you kiss on the first date?

52% Yes
48% No

YOUR FIRST BF

Whether your BGF becomes your BF or ya finally snagged your crush, your first boyfriend is a big deal. After all, you've gotten over the first big hurdle of teen dating: finding a cool guy who's way worthy of you. But here comes that second hurdle: knowing the secrets of being the GF he can't wait to hang out with.

♥ Silence is golden

One of the biggest mistakes a new GF can make? Blabbing to the gang about the mushy text messages he sends you, how he goes out of his way to walk you to soccer practice, and the funny little IM exchange you two had last night. Of course, it's all wonderful and adorable, but . . .

The truth is, most guys don't like their love lives becoming fodder for gossip sessions. Once he catches wind of your loose-lip fests, he'll likely be less than happy about it. So keep those details on the DL.

♥ Let freedom ring

As much as you like being alone with your guy, you two will be spending hang time with his crew, too. Nobody says you have to like them all, but they're his buddies so be pleasant, at the very least.

That said, you don't want to be the constant tag-along gal. Just like you and your friends enjoy a girls' night out, your boyfriend deserves to have guy-bonding time. Don't take his wanting to hang with the guys as rejection. It's actually healthy for couples to do things apart from each other. Besides, if you spend every waking moment with your boy, you two are bound to get bored.

♥ Stay true to you

Changing for a BF is bad, bad, bad. **If he's really a good guy, he should like you for who you are.** A guy who pressures you to lose weight or put on more makeup or wear different clothes isn't worth a minute of your time. This is not to say he can't make suggestions ("You're really cute in that red halter."), but your personal style is ultimately up to you.

Also, don't pretend to be someone you're not. Don't tell him you're an avid water-skier if you can barely stay float.

You'll wind up drowning in the deceit when he's eventually onto you. If he turns you on to something that genuinely interests you, great. You never knew baseball was such a blast? You two can munch nachos together while watching the World Series.

No need to be needy

Yes, you adore him. But your new guy doesn't define who you are, and you definitely don't need him. **A guy can tire very quickly of a girl who follows him around like a puppy** and hangs on his every move. He'll have loads more respect and find you much more attractive if you show him that you have your own goals and passions in life.

Guys like girls who are confident with themselves and can blaze their own trails. Don't leave him ten messages in one day and expect him to be thrilled about it. In fact, that can be just plain scary. If he's unavailable for the moment, leave it at that and find something else to do (besides sitting by the phone waiting for a return call, please).

♥ Think like a guy

As in, live for the moment. Girls tend to fantasize about the future while guys . . . don't. Telling him how much you're looking forward to the months-away Christmas dance, while he's looking forward to a cheesesteak at lunch, is a recipe for disaster.

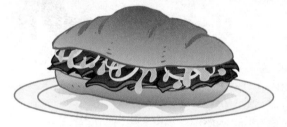

The trick is not to obsess or set yourself up for disappointment. Enjoy your time with him, and take it lightly. Instead of gushing about twirling under the mistletoe, do the guy thing and chat about what DVD to rent tonight. Keep the drama on your TV, or you might hear these two words: The End.

HELP!

"I want to be friends with boys, without them staring at me and wondering why I'm hanging out with them. How can I do that?"

GL SAYS . . .

There are some rules for striking up a friendship with a guy. The first may be a no-brainer, but don't flirt: no complimenting his muscles or rifling your fingers through his hair. The next rule—finding something in common—is true for all friendships, but it's easier if you both dig a certain band, love the same sport, or are members of the debate team. The last rule is to be yourself but remember that guy friends don't necessarily care to discuss the latest chick flicks or spend three hours at the mall . . . so save that for girl time.

Get Cling-Free!

Do you need to give your BF a little breathing room?
See if you fit any of these clinger profiles. . . .

● ● ● ● ● ● ● ● ● ● ● ● ● ● ● ● ● ●

✻ The Boa Constrictor

If you're constantly wrapped around your boyfriend's neck when he's trying to hang with his crew, you're probably making him—and them—really uncomfortable. So keep PDA to a minimum around a guy's crew. Playing it low-key around his circle shows you're laid-back and confident.

✻ The Adoring Fan

It's great to tell your boyfriend how much you dig him . . . but if you lay it on too thick, you send the wrong message. Plus, even the most solid guy ever can get a swollen ego from all that fawning. Save the flattery for when you really mean it. Besides, you've already paid him the best compliment ever . . . by agreeing to be his girl.

✻ The Text Offender

You send him an update in the A.M., after class, at lunch, before dinner, then . . . Sure, your guy likes to hear about your day. But a little space is always a good thing, so relish time away from each other. When you get the urge to text, call a friend instead.

✻ The Drop-Everything Gal

It's normal to want to spend lots of time with your guy. But if you're hanging with him at the expense of everything else, take a step back. Don't rearrange your world to be with your guy. It's tempting to make him your No. 1 priority, but having outside interests is what makes you, well, you.

TROUBLE IN PARADISE

Sure, having a BF can be awesome: You've got an automatic date for the dance. Someone to share that bucket of buttery popcorn with at the movies. The fluttery feeling you get when he looks at you. But then again, relationships aren't always so wonderful. Of course there are those guys who belong in the Bad Boyfriend Hall of Fame (you know who he is). But sometimes, your BF isn't even a bad guy—he's just bad *for you*. Here are some not so obvious reasons to kiss your guy good-bye.

◆ GO SOLO SIGN #1: You're just not that into him

Your BF clearly adores you: He hangs on your every word, surprises you with sweet treats, texts you constantly just to say, "i miss u!" Only prob? You don't quite have the same feelings for him. And though the constant flattery can be nice, it can also get overwhelming when you're not, well, sharing the love. So spare your sensitive sweetie any future heartache by halting things now. He'll find another girl to gush over, and you'll have the freedom to seek someone who really makes you melt.

◆ GO SOLO SIGN #2: You're with him for the wrong reasons

It's not easy being the lone single girl in your group of friends or the only one who's never had a boyfriend. But settling for a guy who's less than stellar just to enter coupledom is not the way to go. While you may be able to say, "I have a boyfriend," *if your heart's not in it, why waste your time and energy?* So evaluate your relationship and figure out if it's really worth it. If not, break things off and take pride in your single status. Besides, being the only solo sister in your crew means more cuties for you!

◆ GO SOLO SIGN #3: You're too busy for a BF

This week, you've got tennis practice, singing lessons, and a babysitting gig. Top that with family obligations and BFF time, and you're left with mere minutes for your guy. As much as you'd like to make things work, *the reality is you just aren't at a place where a BF is a priority.* And that's OK. There will be a right time for a guy—it's just not today.

◆ GO SOLO SIGN #4: You're out of his league

Burping the alphabet may have been funny when you were, like, 5. And slinging insults at underclassmen reeks of playground nonsense that was never actually amusing at all. *So if your BF's bordering on immature,* realize you can do better. In a few years, maybe he'll be worth another date. But for right now, let him keep kidding around while you find a guy who's a little more grown up.

✦ GO SOLO SIGN #5: You're bored

Another Friday, another Netflix night with your BF. Yawn. *Maybe the smoke from those initial sparks has started to clear* and the two of you don't have so much in common after all. Before you give up, suggest you do something different on your next date (bowling, a hike, whatever isn't the usual). If you still find yourself thinking about doing anything but spending time with your sweetie, take that as a major sign that it's time to turn this guy loose.

✦ GO SOLO SIGN #6: You're majorly crushing on other guys

OK, it's not like you have to turn off your cute-guy radar. But if you are wishing and hoping that the math genius in your algebra class will finally put two and two together and realize you are, uh, "four" him, it's time to bid your fella farewell. *Even though you do like him, it's not really fair, is it?* So say, "Let's just be friends" (in a nice way!), and mean it. That way, you can keep crushing—and you're free to date someone you really like.

BREAKING UP

And when it's time to go your own way? We won't lie to you—breakups are never fun. But know that it is possible to let him down without breaking his (and your) heart. Here are some tips that might help ease the pain for both of you.

✷ Keep it quiet

Before you go gabbing to your crew, the whole soccer league, and half your class, think about how not fun it is to hear that you are about to get dumped! Breaking news of the breakup is something your boyfriend should hear straight from the source—you. Sure, rely on your closest friends for support, but don't let them do your dirty work.

✷ Location, location, location

Don't dump your BF in front of an audience. Ideally, you should be bold and tell him face-to-face, but have a heart and do it when you two are alone. If you can't find some one-on-one time, it's fine to tell him over the phone. But even though this is the age of technology, it's not cool to dump him over IM or e-mail.

✷ Honesty is the best policy

You spend a week making up some story you think will soften the blow, and the best you can come up with is, "I can't date you anymore, Henry, because, umm . . . my great-aunt twice removed has acid reflux so I'll be

spending a lot of time with her."
Whatever, Pinocchio! Steer
clear of lying. He'll respect you
a whole lot
more if you
are up-front.

A simple,
"I don't
think we're
compatible
as a couple,"
will do.
No further
explanation
or drama
needed.

✱ Boys have feelings, too

Your boyfriend (now ex) might
be sad or angry (or both)
about the breakup. That's to be
expected. Don't be surprised if
you wind up feeling a little low,
too. Give yourselves some time
to bounce back before jumping
on the "we can be friends" ship.
Ending a relationship is never
easy—even when it's your idea.

HELP!

"I'm not ready to take that next step with a guy!"

GL SAYS . . .

Whether it's a BGF
makin' a move on you
or your boyfriend
trying to take things
to the next level,
do not feel silly for
shying away from
anything that makes
you feel pressured or
uncomfortable. Your
first instinct is usually
accurate. If it's telling
you that this isn't
right, don't do it.

DEALING WITH GETTING DUMPED

And what if the breakup isn't your idea? Well, we don't have to tell you that being dumped sucks. Big-time. When you're dropped by a guy you genuinely liked, it can feel like your world—and your heart—has been completely shattered. It's gonna take some effort on your part to move on to the next chapter of your personal crush manual. But, in time, your wounds will heal (swear!).

⦾ Let yourself cry

Breaking up is sort of like someone passing away. **You need to allow yourself to mourn** the end of the relationship and cherish the good times while they lasted.
So grab a box of tissues and cry your heart out.

⦾ Throw a pity party

Invite your besties over for a girls-only, all-night pajama party complete with chick flicks, pizza, ice cream, and popcorn. After all, that's what pals are for—**to pick you up when you're feeling down.**

⊚ Change your relationship status

Everyone knows it's not official until it's on Facebook. **This is an important step in letting go.** If you don't want everyone to know your business, change your privacy settings before you update your profile.

• •

⊚ Don't stalk him

No, you don't have permission to cybercreep on his every move. **And yeah, it's gonna be hard to resist** checking out those new pics of him from the weekend. Unfriend him, block him, or take his number out of your phone if temptation is too much.

• •

⊚ Sweat it out

Exercise is a great way to release stress. **And what's more stressful than a big breakup?** You're probably feeling angry, so sign up for a cardio kickboxing class. Engage yourself in a high-impact workout to free your mind and get your body moving in a good way.

• •

⊚ Treat yourself

Remember that cute pair of flats you've had your eye on for weeks? Or those gorgeous earrings at the mall? Now's the time to buy 'em for a little pick-me-up. **Just be careful not to break the bank.** Limit yourself to one cheapie fave that makes you look gorgeous.

⊚ Laugh out loud

It's fun. It burns calories. And it makes you look oh-so-attractive. What's not to heart? Watch your fave funny flick for inspiration and let the good times roll.

· ·

⊚ Flirt like crazy

Why not? **You're a sassy single sistah ready to mingle.** Flirting is fun and it's a total confidence booster. Start by smiling at the cutie at the next table in the caf. When he smiles back and strikes up a convo, you'll forget about your ex in no time.

· ·

⊚ Enjoy your solo time

The last thing you want to do is rush into another relationship. **Take a breather to relax** and think about your last one. What went wrong? What was right? And what can you improve next time? Every BF gives ya a chance to love and learn.

THE BOTTOM LINE . . .

Sure, love can be a wonderful thing, but it's also super-complicated (just ask your bud who's buggin' about her BF 24/7). So, whether you're recently broken up with your BF or you're just not ready to date, know that being single makes ya stronger. After all, you don't need a guy to tell you how ridiculously awesome you are. You know you're smart, fun, and beautiful. The right fella will come along who truly appreciates you for simply being you.

Stressin' Less at School

3

School's a huge source of drama in your world because, well, you spend so darn much of your time there. And between balancing all of the tests, papers, and projects with pleasing your teach *and* staying in touch with your crew, it's **easy to feel freaked** here and there.

But school doesn't have to be such a stress. Whether it's handling challenges in the classroom or keeping up with your crew, here's how to tackle the toughest sitches so that *school can be a blast*—not a burden!

The Time Crunch

Quizzes, papers, and projects . . . oh, my! You're totally overwhelmed—and feeling over-your-head anxious about academics. What to do when work piles up and time dwindles down? Organization is key. Start by following these steps and your school year will be golden, girl!

✦ See it!

If you've got a lot of work due, make a big list arranged by due dates. That way you can visually see what you've got going on. Hang it up in your room so you can always see what's next. Or get a calendar and color code each of your classes. Geography is green, French is pink, science is orange, and so on. You could also carry around a daily planner. Experiment with a few different methods or use 'em all at once.

✦ Timeline

You're a busy girl with field hockey, school, and homework, but you shouldn't be up late doing work every night. If your project is due in two weeks, break it up. There's no need to finish the whole thing in two days, especially if you have other stuff to get done, too. Work on it a little bit each night, and you will get the entire thing done well before it's due.

✦ Prioritize

If you've got a lot of homework one night and a big project due next week, don't start the proj. Do your homework for tomorrow and leave your project for a night where you're less busy, or even the weekend. Got a few great ideas and afraid you'll run out of creative juice fast? Give yourself twenty or so minutes to write 'em down, then get back on track for the stuff due ASAP.

Make sure the environment you're doing your work in is free of distractions. Hang in your bedroom with your Internet off, your phone far away, and some music that makes you feel productive. Break up your load subject by subject, and tackle the hardest stuff first when your energy is still high. You need to complete your week effectively and efficiently, not plow through it all in one night.

Growing girls need about eight hours of sleep a night, so it's important that you get a good amount of shut-eye. *Try to get to bed by the same time every night*, that way you are well-rested for the next day and ready to take on your busy schedule. If you organize your time, cut back on distractions, and prioritize, you won't find yourself up til all hours.

TOUGH-ON-YA TEACHERS

Phew! It's hard enough to handle all of that homework, but having a teach who treats ya unfairly can make school seriously stressful. Whether you feel like she never calls on you when you raise your hand, or she's super-hard on you, it's pretty common to think your teacher doesn't like you. But the good news is, you should be able to get Teach to change her 'tude—if you go about it the right way.

◉ Figuring it out

First, be honest with yourself and think about anything that you could be doing that is bugging your teacher. *Are you a notorious note passer?* Gum chewer? Do you sneak texts to your BFF while you're supposed to be working on math probs? Then she may be *annoyed* by these acts. And of course, if she caught ya lying, cheating, cutting class, or copying someone else's homework, she'll

63

be disappointed in your dishonesty. If she saw you making fun of or mistreating another kid, she may put you in the *class bully* category.

If you've landed on her bad side, the obvs answer is to stop doin' what you're doing. *Then, start making a big effort to show ya truly really care about class.* Raise your hand whenever you can. Be nicer, more helpful, and more involved in class and after school. Pay more attention and ask questions when you don't understand. Your new attitude will prove you can be a good student—and hopefully, your teacher will lighten up on you.

But if you're staying on the straight-and-narrow in class and your teacher still isn't giving you the grades or treatment you deserve,

don't be afraid to approach her. Take some time after school and say, "I don't know what I've done, but I get the feeling you are angry with me." Don't accuse her of anything; simply wait for her to explain her recent behavior toward you. If you're OK with her answer, *it is possible you can work together on improving your relationship.* But if, after your talk, you still feel she can't be nice to you, talk to your parents or a guidance counselor about other options.

Opening up

If the sitch is more serious—say, you're super-sad about troubles at home and you're *having a hard time concentrating* in class—tell your teacher. Because though he may be smart, he's not a psychic. He'll take your bad mood for just that—and will assume you don't like him or the way he teaches.

Confide in your teacher about it one day after school. Whether you've had a fight with your mom or a family member is ill, *your teacher will be glad to know the real reason you have been so out of it.* He may even give you extra time to catch up on your studies. (But don't even think of making something up to get out of a tough spot—teachers always know when you lie and then you'll really be in deep.)

⦿ Dealing with it

And if none of these solutions do the trick? *Let's face it—some personalities don't mix.* If vibes between you and your teacher aren't perfect, don't take it as an insult. It doesn't mean you're weird or unlikable. *Teachers, like students, come in all flavors:* strict, fun, mean, friendly, geeky, cool. Instead of worrying about why you're not the favorite, learn as much as you can and make friends with other kids.

The Friend Factor

We covered tonsa topics about your friends in Chapter One, but stuff that happens at school can spark some big-time drama between buds. After all, in an ideal world, you and your BFF would be in every class together—including lunch—and laugh your way through the day. Most of the time, though, your crew gets split up in school, or other things happen—you develop new interests or meet new peeps—that can challenge a friendship. Here's how to stay on track when pal potholes pop up in school.

One of you gets a boyfriend

The excitement of getting a new boyfriend is even better than walking into an afternoon class and seeing a substitute! But a guy takes time and attention away from buds. How will you deal?

If it's you: When he asks if you feel like meeting him at the game on Saturday, will you ask your BFF to come along? Or will you just conveniently forget the fact that you always spend Saturdays with her? Now is the time to compromise and make plans with your new guy and your BFF (and keep those plans, no matter what!). Put it this way: Let's say this boy is around for a month. Will your friend be around if you practically ditch her for the entire thirty days?

If it's her:
It's hard not to feel jealous. But don't confuse her excitement for him as a sign that you're now not important in her world. Also key:

Resist judging her new situation, be happy for her, and let her talk about and enjoy her new romance (you'd want the same if things were reversed).

One of you becomes popular.

Certain things can propel a girl from wallflower to homecoming queen: showing up after summer break looking like a supermodel, making the cheerleading squad, dating the hottest guy in the grade above you, whatever. Sudden popularity can cause a big shift among sistahs. What do you do?

If it's you: Your friend is your friend, and becoming popular just equals *more* friends, not *replacement* friends. If you want to rank and categorize people based on their popularity, you'll be all alone at the top. Introduce your new buds to your BFF and, whatever you do, keep it real.

If it's her: This sitch can feel like you're standing in your friend's shadow. If she gets a little big-headed, it's likely just a temporary ballooning of her ego, so try not to be too annoyed while you wait it out. If she starts ditching you, remind her of who was there when she, say, accidentally peed her pants in the third grade. Chances are the attention will fade, and you'll be back to good soon enough.

One of you is NOT invited to a party.

It's the party of the year! Everyone will be there—but for whatever reason, one of you has an invite, and the other does not.

If it's you: Did the hostess confuse your locker number? It's a good bet that there's a logical reason for your friend getting invited and not you. But if you were definitely left off the list, go ahead and make alternative plans for that night. Chances are your BFF will feel guilty about going, but show her you know it's not her fault you weren't invited. And if she does go? Make your pal promise she'll give you all the gossip as soon as she gets home!

If it's her: Yes, you want to go to this party. But it won't be nearly as fun without your BFF. So call the hostess and ask her if by chance your BFF's invite got lost. If she says she wasn't invited, thank the hostess for including you on her guest list, but then decline politely. You've got other plans. Such as? Spending an evening with the coolest girl in town—your BFF.

● ● ● ● ● ●

One of you moves away.

Whether it's to the other side of town or the other side of the country, a physical separation is a brutal hurdle for a friendship to clear. Can you stay close when you're so far away?

If it's you: Maintaining a long-distance friendship takes lots and lots of effort, but that's why e-mail, text, and Facebook exist! Keep in touch by checking in regularly.

If it's her: Even though it's not her fault, it's hard not to feel like your BFF abandoned you. Your No. 1 hang is hauling her stuff away, so what are you supposed to do now? Step one: Have a going-away party! Any excuse for a bash is a good excuse! Step two: Make plans for long, quality visits. Step three: Promise to stay in close touch. Step four: Stay in touch!

Dealing With Mean Girls

So maybe it's not friends or teachers that have got ya buggin'. Maybe it's something so much harder to remedy: You're being bullied. You can't walk into the caf without the Queen of Mean LOL'ing at your outfit or whispering with her crew while looking directly at you. Being victimized by a bully can

be downright heartbreaking—not to mention damaging to your performance in school, sports, and anything else you're involved in. So how do you deal when someone's making your life miserable? Aside from permanently hibernating?

✴ Stay Yourself

First off, never change yourself in an effort to make a mean girl accept you. Truth is, you could make over your entire being and she probably still wouldn't like you. Why? Because she doesn't want to—she's already made up her mind on this. *Just be yourself.* So what if she isn't feeling you? Do you really want to be buds with someone who treats people so viciously, anyway? *Focus instead on your fabulous friends* who adore and accept you exactly as you are.

✴ Strip Away Her Power

Every time you let her upset you, you add fuel to her fire—so stop! Next time she approaches, rather than be intimidated, show her you can hold your own. *Look her directly in the eye* when you talk to her. This simple yet powerful act lets her know you're on equal ground. Keep your composure, speak with conviction, and exude loads of confidence. By putting on a fearless face and confronting her head-on, you'll realize she's not all-powerful. Underneath those evil layers, *she's just a girl,* same as you.

✴ Take It as a Compliment

Sounds strange, but for some reason, you've clearly had a major influence on this miserable mama. It could be that *she feels threatened* by you, so she feels the need to tear you down. If she really thought you were a loser, she wouldn't waste her precious breath. She probably sees you as a force to be reckoned with. So her meanness is a feeble attempt at *maintaining authority* and assuring you don't steal her coveted throne. So rather than letting her agitate you, feel flattered that she considers you important enough to torment.

✴ Feel Sorry for Her

Almost all bullies are *severely lacking self-confidence,* and likely the one targeting you is no exception. *Since she doesn't believe in herself,* she thinks the only way people will hang with her is if she coerces them into it. She knows if her underlings are rattled by her, *they'll do what she says.* Sad, isn't it? But this should help you understand that it's about her shortcomings, not yours. She has major self-esteem deficiency. Next time she does something rotten, feel bad for her that *her insecurities make her act like such a jerk.*

✳ Be the Bigger Person

Although she gives you so much attention, show her you definitely don't deem her worthy of yours by refusing to be rude in response. After all, you have *far better things* to concentrate on. Not only will you *impress people* by caring so little about Miss Wicked's ways, but your pride will skyrocket from knowing you held your own. *Nothing infuriates a mean girl more* than when her loathsome actions go ignored and un-avenged. This shows her she didn't accomplish her goal of inflicting pain or embarrassment.

Now that you realize she has no control over you, she can hurl as many insults as she wants. Because you're immune. She was right to be threatened by you—you have the ability to end her reign as Queen Witchiness!

THE BOTTOM LINE . . .

School may not be your favorite thing in the whole wide world, but the hours you spend in those hallways and classrooms definitely shape you as a sistah. From the teachers you learn from to the friends you lean on, the relationships you develop in school will give you plenty of life-lessons that can help ya big-time when facing challenges in the future. Keep your friendships fab and your attitude awesome—and you'll soar like the superstar you were born to be!

Other Ways to Bring Down a Bully

☀ **Ignore, ignore**

Bullies just want to see you suffer. If you pretend the bully doesn't exist, it takes away his or her power over you.

☀ **Keep your emotions in check**

This can be really challenging, but don't cry, shout, or get upset in the presence of bullies. Keep it together and they'll learn you aren't an easy target.

☀ **Go the other way**

Remove yourself from unhealthy situations. Go in the opposite direction, preferably toward a crowd where there are adults present.

☀ **Safety in numbers**

You're less likely to get picked on when you're surrounded by others.

☀ **Find new friends**

If your best buds are bad news, start looking for some new friends. It's not easy, but joining new activities and finding things to do outside of school is a good start.

☀ **Get a confidence boost**

Sign up for music lessons, try a new sport, get a part-time babysitting gig. Start participating in something that makes you feel good about yourself.

☀ **Don't blame yourself**

Always remember it's not your fault.

☀ **Seek support**

Tell your parents, a teacher, a counselor, or a coach. If you feel uncomfortable talking about it, write them a letter. People who are bullied often need help. Don't be afraid to ask for it.

Family Matters

Sure, you love your fam: They laugh at all of your jokes, let you slide when you do something mega-mortifying, and are almost always there when you really need 'em (admit it, you wouldn't have aced that geography bee if your fam wasn't sitting front-row in the audience, waving signs made just for you).

But then there are those moments that make you wish for replacement relatives—you know, some that aren't so embarrassing/strict/totally uncool. And although the 'rents may make ya want to scream with their strict rules and the sibs may drive you up the wall with their whining, thing is, we can just about guarantee that you'll be super-thankful for them a li'l ways down the road of life. So here's how to deal in the meantime!

Wish you were here!

STRICTLY BUSINESS

From taking away your text time to banishing boys, it may seem like your parents are on a mission to mess up your life—but chances are, they're just lookin' out for you. So while you have to respect their rules, that's not to say you can't bend them a bit by working with your 'rents so they loosen up on their laws.

CURFEW CLASH

> **"I'm the only one of my friends who has to be home by 9:00 P.M. Everyone else can stay out til at least 10:30. I keep telling my parents that I'm missing everything, but they won't back down!"**

YOUR 'RENTS' REASONING: The root of this rule lies in your parents' fear of the unknown. As in, they get spooked when they don't know what you're doing when you're away from home. A lot can happen when you're out and about, so your 'rents are gonna worry unless you're home, safe 'n' sound—preferably in your PJs on the couch.

BEND IT A BIT: The easiest way to conquer the curfew clash? Offer up legit reasons for why you need to stay out later—are you and your buds planning to see a 7:30 movie? Hitting up the diner after the football game? If your parents are completely clear on where you are and when, they may be more open to letting you hang a little later. Then, take baby steps toward an extended curfew by first asking if you can stay out for an extra half hour one night a week. If they say OK, stick to that sched like glue for at least a month before requesting a revision. By showing your 'rents that you respect the clock (and them!), they just may relent to even more time.

TIGHT LEASH

"My parents don't let me go anywhere. If I want to do anything that's not planned, they flip out. They don't want me to have a life!"

YOUR 'RENTS' REASONING: Here's a shocker: Your parents definitely want you to have a life—and a great one at that. But they may be micromanaging your time because they think you need to focus less on fun and more on serious stuff, like school and extracurriculars.

BEND IT A BIT: Give your 'rents reasons to relax about your status in school. Get involved, study hard, and keep 'em posted on your progress. And practice the art of good timing: After you spill good news about acing an algebra exam, casually mention that blowout next Friday. Give the 'rents advanced warning about your plans, and they should be so stoked about your score that they'll push you to that party!

TECHNO NO-NO

"My parents are way uptight about all things tech. I can't take my laptop up to my room. I can't have a Facebook page. And though I have a cell phone, no texting!"

YOUR 'RENTS' REASONING: Sure, it sucks to be silenced when it seems like your friends are chattin' and textin' up a storm. But lotsa girls have run into mega-mischief and even danger thanks to technology (do we really need to remind you that there are tons of scary creeps lurking online?).

BEND IT A BIT: Try compromising. Promise to keep your daily calls, texts, and time online to an agreed-upon number. Give your parents open access to your laptop so they can see the websites you're frequenting. Even letting them look at your Facebook profile may put them at ease. And if that doesn't work? Well, as your 'rents will surely remind you, you're not gonna die from going gadgetless—they definitely didn't!

CLOTHES CONTROL

> "My mom won't let me wear what I want. She's totally against anything even remotely short or tight—and forget about tank tops! Plus, I'm not allowed to wear makeup even though I'm in eighth grade."

YOUR 'RENTS' REASONING:
As hot as you may look in those microminis and tight tops, no parent wants to see their girl flashin' so much skin. Or piling on major makeup, for that matter. Plus, super-flirty styles can send mixed (read: wrong) messages to others, especially to guys. And why would you wanna do that?

BEND IT A BIT: Although this may be a battle between you and your parents until you're way into adulthood, there are some ways to soften up those super-strict wardrobe and makeup rules. For starters, give 'em some say in the selection. Suggest a shopping spree with your mom or dad. While you're at it, swing by the makeup counter for a quick consultation. Once your mom sees how that bronze eye shadow brings out your eyes, she just may start letting you sport the shade. But be warned: No matter what, your 'rents are always gonna think you're gorge without makeup. And guess what? You are!

TUNED OUT

"I can't download music without my parents checking the song to make sure it's 'appropriate.' And there are certain shows that I'm not allowed to watch, even though I read books much worse than that!"

YOUR 'RENTS' REASONING: Sure, you may think you're ready to be exposed to anything you want when it comes to television, movies, and music. But entertainment that's geared toward grown-ups (and yeah, teens, too) often comes with attitudes about sex, drugs, and violence that may conflict with your family's values.

BEND IT A BIT: Sick of secretly watching PG-13 rated movies at your BFF's house? Try to get your 'rents to reassess their reasons for keeping tabs on your tunes and TV. Chat with them about what it is they find inappropriate. Then curb any concerns they may have by letting them know you won't let that stuff influence you—and be sure to keep that promise. Asking if they want to watch or listen with you is also another solution. Just be prepared to squirm if and when any awkwardness arises (like, um, during steamy makeout scenes!).

HOW TO TELL YOUR PARENTS ANYTHING

So that's the gist of getting the 'rents to reason with ya. But what about talking to them about other stuff, like the awkward, uncomfy topics that'll surely sprout up? Like if you just got busted cheating on the history exam and you're flipping out!

There is nothing more nerve-racking than having to bring up a tough subject with your parents. How will they react? Are you headed for lecture city? Will they give you tons of unwanted advice, or just think you're being "silly"? Will you be sorry afterward because telling them something actually made the situation worse?

Surely, you've struggled over whether or not you should tell your parents stuff, what you should say, and how you should say it to avoid backlash. No easy task. But here's how to spill so you and your parents can actually feel good about how you handle touchy conversations from now on. Really.

❀ STEP ONE: Be prepared!

First, be clear about what you hope to accomplish. Do you want to ask a simple question, confess, discuss a situation in exquisite detail, or register a complaint? By going into a conversation with crystal-clear objectives, you're more likely to get what you want—because Mom and Dad won't be confused, either.

So ask yourself some questions: "Do I want their opinion?" "Do I just want to get this off my chest?" "Do I want them to help me?"

Second, make sure you're completely calm and level-headed before approaching your parents. That way, you'll think more clearly. Getting overly emotional or overreacting will divert their attention away from what you're trying to say.

Third, prepare yourself by imagining how your mom or dad is likely to react. Be realistic. If Mom typically has a short fuse and you're on the hot seat, brace yourself and acknowledge her feelings. Like, if you're confronting your mom about the crystal vase you broke during a spontaneous dance party with your buds, say something like, "I know you're going to be really mad, and I don't blame you at all." By saying this, you'll

let Mom know you took your mistake seriously.

While most parents are pretty cool and understanding, some have a tendency to get a little freaked or suspicious. An innocent question about, let's say, alcohol, might provoke your dad to ask, "Why are you asking about THAT? Are you drinking?" So you might want to anticipate this reaction by saying, "This has nothing to do with me, but I'm just curious about . . ."

❋ STEP TWO: Spit it out.

Although many girls are masters at putting stuff off, we strongly advise you to *take a deep breath and just spell it out* for the 'rents. If you feel incredibly guilty, putting off a discussion with your mom or dad only makes you feel way worse—and for a longer period of time.

So don't wait for the perfect time to tell them. There isn't one. Say Mom's doing dishes. Interrupt her by politely saying, "Excuse me. Is there any way you could stop what you're doing and talk to me?" If your sibs are nearby, say, "Is it possible for us to talk privately?" Any time you need an opening line, try the most direct one, "Mom, I need to talk to you about something important."

STEP THREE: Do some damage control.

If you're genuinely sorry for something you did, be sure to tell your parents that. *They may not forgive you immediately,* but an apology could soften their anger. Offering to make up for what you did can also go a long way. If you broke your Dad's iPod touch, offer to chip in babysitting bucks to replace it.

If things don't go as well as you had hoped when asking for a special privilege, don't immediately give up unless you're certain you can't win this one. Stay calm, and try again to explain how you feel. Restate your request and the reasons behind it, and maybe you can come up with a compromise.

❋ ONCE THE DEED IS DONE . . .

You always hope your parents will react precisely the way you wanted them to. But if their response isn't what you were hoping for, suggest you all take a little time to think about everything you said. *Just know that the more you talk things over,* the better you'll get at speaking your mind and starting up an open line of convo between you and your 'rents. And although you may not always agree with them, your ability to share your feelings or talk things out reasonably with the 'rents will make you closer. Promise!

DEALING WITH DAD

You may have one of those awesome relationships with your 'rents where you already open up to them about everything. Or maybe, you're much more comfy with confiding stuff in your mom, as most girls are. But what about dear ol' Dad? Not too tight with him? *Well guess what: He's actually got a lot to offer, if you'll let him.* We totally understand that as you become more of an adult and less of a little girl, things between you and Dad can get, well, awkward. Here's how to steer you through some potentially difficult sitches so you and Daddy Dearest can be closer than ever.

● ● ● ● ●

Papa Prob: You have nothing in common! He's a sports nut; you love the arts. He's into action-adventure flicks; you're all about indies. And the list goes on. . . .

DADVICE: Having different interests d[...] you and your dad have to lead separate lives[...] just the two of you can do: Suggest signing up for guitar lessons at the local community college (most offer non-credit classes). Or get into doing crosswords together. Whatever you pick, make sure it's something you're both new to so you'll learn at the same speed. Then, you can talk about your shared activity, which will lead to other conversation topics, too. Voilà! Now you have something in common.

Papa Prob: That cutie from the baseball team asked you out, but your parents want to meet him first. You're sure Dad is going to be mega-intimidating, meaning this may be your first—and last—date.

DADVICE: Your dad is never going to be crazy about the thought of you dating, period. But you can try to make the situation go smoother by prepping both guys for the impending meet-and-greet. Talk to your dad openly about your new guy (just don't gush—that's a little TMI for Dad!). And also give your date the 411 on your dad ("He seems scary, but he's really a softie at heart!"). Figure out what the two have in common (Are they both crazy for baseball? Love outdoors?), then keep the conversation flowing by chatting about that subject when your date arrives. Even the most social boys clam up in the presence of an overprotective papa.

● ● ● ● ● ●

Papa Prob: **You talk to your mom about everything. Your dad? Not so much. But you're in major crisis mode, and Dad's the only one around to confide in. Eek. . . .**

DADVICE: Sure, it's only natural for you to gravitate to your mom for comfort and advice—who else can offer the whole been-there-done-that vibe? But let's not forget Dad's been-there-done-that, too, but only as a guy! And he may be able to offer you some insight. So when your troubles reach a boiling point, ask your dad if he has a few minutes to talk. Even if it's a bit odd at first to chat about such personal stuff, listen up for the valuable things he has to say.

● ● ● ● ● ●

Papa Prob: **You and your dad used to spend tons of time together. But now, between swim team, piano lessons, and weekends with friends, you barely see him.**

DADVICE: Of course your dad wants you to stay busy—and happy. But he's probably also silently wishing you'd pass on chilling with your BFF for the fiftieth time this week and hang with him instead. So add a block of time into your sched for dear ol' Dad: Think about starting a Sunday morning tradition of cooking up fabulous breakfasts together (just make sure you cook enough for the rest of the fam, too). Or earmark Thursday nights for a foosball tourney followed by ice cream sundaes. It's cool if you have to bail when something super-important comes up, but aiming for regular together time can bring a bonus boost to your bond with Dad.

Papa Prob: You're totally responsible and reliable, but your dad still treats you like a baby. He insists on checking your homework each night, and you can't make any plans without him giving you the third degree.

DADVICE: Your dad's been there for you from day one. And naturally, it's gonna be hard for him to let go of his little girl. But to make life easier for both of you, he has to loosen the reins. Sit him down and tell him you're ready to handle things like homework on your own. Promise to provide regular updates on your progress in each class. And as for him wanting to know where you are and who you're with 24/7, earn his trust by offering him honest info before he even asks. Of course he's always going to be super-protective of you—that's just a dad thing.

DECODING DAD

Think Pop's being unfair or just doesn't understand you? Here are some Dad-isms—translated.

He Says: "Do you think I'm made of money?"

He Means: "I would love to give you everything you want, but that's just not possible. I hope you'll learn to appreciate what you have and how to be responsible with money."

He Says: "Don't make me ask you again."

He Means: "I don't want to be the bad guy, but you need to be respectful. We all have responsibilities that we don't necessarily like to deal with—that's life."

He Says: "You'll thank me when you're older."

He Means: "Believe it or not, I was your age once and I've been through similar situations. My experiences can help me to guide you—trust me on this one."

He Says: "Go ask your mother."

He Means: "It's not that I don't care, but I'm a little out of my league here. This is something your mom should weigh in on, too, so we can make a decision together."

THE SIB SITCH

From your big sis always dissin' ya to your bratty bro badmouthing your every move, if you've got siblings, you've got drama. And even though you'd like to jump ship and join another family from time to time, reality is you're stuck with 'em. But that doesn't mean you're stuck with the constant chaos, too. Here's the scoop on solving the most common sibling sitches so you can start remedying those rivalries right away.

ODD GIRL OUT

THE SITCH: With your older sis shining in school and your baby bro always soaking up oodles of extra attention, you can't seem to get any props from your parents.

THE SCOOP:

Whether you're the oldest, the youngest, or smack dab in the middle, it's easy to feel like the forgotten one in the fam. And even though it seems like you're being shortchanged, we promise your parents love each of you equal amounts. They're probably just preoccupied and trust that you can handle things without their constant interference (which is really a compliment to your maturity. Go, you!).

THE SOLUTION: If you want some extra time with your 'rents, speak up and ask for it. Schedule a standing Saturday morning bagel run with Dad or ask Mom if she wants to take a knitting class with you. Use that together time to talk about stuff that's important to you—you'll feel way closer to both parents and won't be so bugged when each of your siblings get their special snaps from them. And know this: All kids feel left out sometimes (even your bro and sis), but your time to shine will come around.

⊚ BAD MOOD BRO

THE SITCH: You and your brother were like besties. But then he hit high school and suddenly he's too busy to hang, or even worse, he doesn't even acknowledge your existence.

THE SCOOP: If your sib is suddenly serving up the silent treatment, chances are he's going through some tough stuff— like all of the pressure that comes along with high school. Maybe he is just feeling insecure or confused by all of the changes in his world and is icing you out as a result.

THE SOLUTION: Try not to take his rude 'tude to heart. Give him some time. The move to high school can be a rough transition for some, but hopefully once he settles in at school, he'll relax and become the bro you know and love again. In the meantime, offer your support by letting him know you're there if he ever wants to chat, to help him work out any probs, or to just be there and be you. That's what sisters are for, right?

⊚ STUCK-ON-YOU SIS

THE SITCH: Your little sis may be sweet, but after hours of her following you around, crashing your slumber parties, and mimicking your every move, she's way more annoying than adorable.

THE SCOOP: Yeah, it may be aggravating to always have her by your side, but all of that attention your sis is showering on ya just shows how much she wants to be like you. Which is pretty flattering when you think about it.

THE SOLUTION: Don't burst her itty-bitty bubble. Suck it up and include her in limited amounts of time with your buds (say, at the start of your next sleepover with your crew, spend an hour scrapbooking together before her bedtime. Then go back to doin' your thing when she hits the hay). And when the Velcro-treatment becomes a tad too much, enlist Mom in your cause: Let her know you're craving a break, and ask her to keep the wee one busy for a bit. Bet you'll actually enjoy the time you spend with sis after some hours apart—and maybe she'll discover there's more to life than following you around.

⊚ CLOSET CREEPER

THE SITCH: You and your sister are finally the same size. Which is great and all—until she starts sneaking in your room and borrowing your best stuff without asking.

THE SCOOP: Let's face it: It's always fun to poke around in someone else's stuff. Especially when that someone is a fab fashionista like you! (After all, as the old saying goes, imitation is the sincerest form of flattery.) Your sis is probably longing to look just like you, but isn't mature enough to ask you outright for permission to borrow your belongings.

THE SOLUTION: Have a heart-to-heart with your sneaky sib. Tell her you'd be cool sharing your stuff with her as long as she asks for it in advance. Point out that you respect her privacy and expect the same. Even if ya share a room, you're each entitled to some personal space. And if she continues to raid your closet, have the 'rents lay down the law: Next time she lifts your cherished cashmere cardigan, she's paying to have it dry-cleaned. Maybe that'll scare her enough that she'll just go out and buy one for herself.

SHADOW SISTER

THE SITCH: People are constantly comparing you to your sister—who just so happens to be the prom queen, the class prez, *and* leading setter on the volleyball team. No matter what, you just never measure up.

THE SCOOP: Stuck in the shadows much? It's hard to compete with the girl who seems to have it all—even harder when she's related to you. Feeling second-rate or even a bit jealous is pretty typical among siblings, especially those close in age.

THE SOLUTION:
Even though it seems like the spotlight's always on your sister, realize that you deserve plenty of praise, too. You may not be an all-star setter. So what? You're supersmart, an awesome singer, and can bake a killer pecan pie. By focusing on your own fab qualities and concentrating on the things you love, you'll lessen all of the pressure you're piling on yourself. And that way, people will see you for the self-confident superstar that you are.

FORCED FAMILY FUN

It's one thing to have to sacrifice all of your Saturdays for Family Fun Night. But now you just found out that your parents have planned a two-week vacay touring all of the nation's national parks. So much for spring break on the beach with your besties! Spending every minute with the dearly-beloveds is, well, not exactly a walk in Yellowstone National Park. But guess what? Whether it's occupying your-self in the car or pleasing the parents so you can have some fun, too, you can definitely deal.

⊙ Be a road (trip) warrior

A car trip to the mall with the fam is bad enough. Hours on end? Not pretty. *Getting there truly is half the battle, so be prepared.* And we're not just talking about a good read. Make sure you can keep everyone else occupied, too. Make a playlist with your bro, then let him borrow your iPod to listen to it. Download a couple kiddie movies from iTunes for your little cousin to watch on your laptop. With a little prep, everyone will be busy, not buggin'.

Make a new plan

Your mom's all about museums, and your dad spends his days casting lines. *Meanwhile, you're left choosing* between yet another boring pottery exhibit or skewering worms on hooks. Time to Google your upcoming vacay spot. Maybe you can talk your mom into a shopping spree at nearby outlets. Or try to get tix to a concert you'd all enjoy. With a little research, you *don't have to settle for ho-hum.*

Set sit limits

You don't mind hangin' with the fam, but last year your vacation was more like babysitting duty 24/7. This year, sit the 'rents down a couple weeks before hitting the road and address the issue. *They probably aren't even aware* of how much they rely on you. Offer to pitch in a few hours every day, but then nicely remind them that it's your vacation, too, so you'll need some personal time.

● Pick your battles

If you're even a minute late, Dad's on the phone givin' the police your vital stats. And last year when you asked to go to the resort's teen dance, your mom was all, "Not a chance." Ugh. *The key is to negotiate now.* Pick three or four things you'd really like to do that take you more than ten feet out of their grasp. You know, like participate in a teen snorkel trip. Tell them why you want to go ("I love the water, and it'll be fun to hang with kids my age!") and maturely address their concerns ("I'll do everything the instructor says, and I promise I'll wear SPF 45!"). You may not get to do everything you want, *but you'll probably win a battle or two.* And that's a start. Happy trails!

THE BOTTOM LINE . . .

Whether you're suffering through an endless summer vacay with 'em or just stuck at home, your family isn't always gonna top your list of fun folks. So yeah, maybe your bro *did* blurt out your crush to all of your friends and yep, it wasn't quite cool for your dad to dis your friend. We're not going to argue that your family has its flaws. But hey—you do, too. We all do. That's what makes us human. And if you take a long look at your loved ones, you'll realize that they do a lot more for you than just make your life difficult. Actually, we bet they're pretty cool peeps. They've gotta be at least a *little* awesome—they're related to you!

The Problem Is Me!

So maybe it's not your fam, friends, teachers, or guys that are throwing a wrench in your world. Rather, you feel like *you're* the one causing all of the drama. Well, don't sweat it too much, missy. Deep down inside, we've all got a little drama queen in us. We're all guilty of saying or doing something that's not quite cool—or, quite frankly, makes us look like a fool.

But don't beat yourself up. Your issues—every last one of 'em!—can be totally resolved with a little work. Whether it's learning to *really* love yourself or curbing your gossip habit, all it takes is some effort on your part, and you'll be well on your way to problem-free.

SLAYING YOUR INNER DEMONS

First things first. The root of so many of our personal probs lie in that icky "I" word: Insecurity. We're all insecure about something or other. Our hair. Our bodies. The way we laugh a little too loud when we're nervous. It's OK to not be crazy about 100 percent of yourself, but the more you focus on your flaws, the less happy you'll be. Study after study says that when you're confident and secure, you're more likely to do better in school, make friends, and deal with disappointments and difficulties.

But with all of the stress and pressure you face every day, it's no shocker that a majority of girls feel insecure or unsure of themselves. What's worse is that girls with low self-esteem are more likely to struggle with an eating disorder, smoke, drink, or face other behavioral issues, like cutting. But as scary as these statistics are, there are plenty of quick and simple ways to help you feel good about yourself. So, if you're in need of a confidence boost (aren't we all?), these seven steps are guaranteed to send your self-esteem soaring.

✳ Be your body's BFF

You know how sometimes you look in the mirror and just don't like what you see starin' back at ya? **Whether it's a ginormous zit on your forehead or the way your jeans are tight in all the wrong places,** we all have those bad-body days. But that doesn't mean you should hide under a hat or in baggy clothes for the rest of the school year. Instead, find whatever it is you do like about your body and show it off. Sure, you may have a zit—but check out how that new skirt shows off your muscular legs! As you flaunt your fab features—and rack up the compliments—you'll forget all about those so-called flaws.

✳ Be positive

Yikes! You totally stumbled through your part of the group presentation. Or maybe you missed a step on the stairs and tripped in front of the class hottie. As much as you want to escape into oblivion after embarrassment, you have to move on. Easier said than done, we know. **But first, realize that everyone has bad days.** Then, try to find the humor in the humiliation. Being able to laugh at yourself shows that you have the confidence to carry on through any mortifying moment.

✳ Be a good friend

You know how you always turn to your best bud whenever you have a problem? Maybe it's the way she listens to your every word or lets you obsess over your crush for hours and hours. Whatever it is that makes your pal perfect, make sure that you are showing her the same love. Ask what's going on in her world. Offer words of support when you know she needs a pick-me-up. **Simple, sweet acts will put a gigantic smile on her face—and make you feel great.** After all, even if you think your relationship's already pretty solid, really being there for your other half will make you feel more whole.

✳ Be a do-gooder

It sounds cliché, but reaching out to those who are less fortunate really does make you feel better about yourself. **So get hooked on helping:** raise funds for your fave cause, visit with an elderly neighbor, tutor a classmate, or go snuggle with puppies at your local animal shelter. Whatever you choose to do, you'll be amazed at how helping others can instantly lift your spirits and give you a sense of purpose.

✳ Be passionate

It's no wonder that girls with low self-esteem are often shy, too. **The two traits go hand in hand** as insecure girls are often too intimidated to introduce themselves to new people. So if you're a shy sistah, upping your esteem can be as simple as stepping out of your comfort zone and trying something new. Love photography? **Register for a summer session at the community college.**

Nuts for knitting? Check out group classes at a nearby sewing shop. Once you get into doing something you're actually passionate about, you'll exude so much confidence that everyone will flock to you.

✳ Be sporty

It's a natural reaction to want to sink into your sofa with a bag of chips whenever your thoughts turn south. **But vegging out can actually make you feel worse.** So fight the urge to flop and get active instead. Even just fifteen minutes of easy exercise will release feel-good hormones called *endorphins*, helping you go from blah to bangin'.

An even better option? Join a team. Studies prove that girls who play sports tend to have higher levels of self-esteem. If you missed your school's soccer tryouts, organize an after-school pickup league in your neighborhood.

✳ Be yourself

So maybe you don't have that one dress that everyone will be sporting this summer. So what? **If you're spending your time comparing yourself to others, well, you're wasting a lot of precious minutes.** Especially when it comes to pricey material possessions—what's in one second will be out the next, so why bother buying it in the first place? And whether it's your eclectic taste in tunes, your funky fashion, or your awesomely out-there sense of humor, **be happy with whatever makes you you.**

LIAR LIAR

Speaking of self-esteem, girls who lack it are more likely to lie in order to impress others. Sure, it's okay to tell a harmless white lie here or there—especially when it comes to protecting pals from unnecessary embarrassment or hurt. Sound familiar? Well, you may not think your "little" lies aren't hurting anyone, but constantly fibbing to seem smarter, cooler, or more successful can quickly spiral out of control—and cause major damage to your relationships with friends and family.

Why do you lie?• • • • • • • • • •

The thing is, chica, your friends want to get to know the real you. *Your parents want to trust the real you.* And as cliché as it may sound, honesty truly is the best policy. First off, try to think about why you're lying. Are you uncomfy 'cause you've changed? Upset since you're not as popular? *Try to think about what types of sitches spark lies and why you could be letting fibs fly.* Keep a journal and jot down what you lie about, when you lie, and how you feel after. Then, make a list of all the true, real reasons why you absolutely rock. Cross out all of your lies or rip 'em up. Put the positive list in a place where you can easily see it *to remind yourself* of the reasons why you should be happy being you.

Lie detector!

It's gonna be hard to break the old habit at first, though. So wear a rubber band and snap it every time you lie to catch yourself in the act. Those first few weeks, it'll be a matter of making yourself tell the truth. When you do lie, counter the lie with a "Just kidding" and force yourself to tell the truth. For a  while, it'll be self-correction, but after a couple weeks, *you'll find yourself lying less and less.* Get your friends to help, too. Tell them to call you out when you start to fabricate or when something just doesn't seem real anymore. With a good core team, you'll get to the bottom of your icky prob.

BIG MOUTHS

So you may not be a liar. In fact, you're a little *too* honest when it comes to 'fessing your feelings and other emotions to friends. And often your big mouth lands ya in hot water more than you like. Whether you're a gossip or tend to let your temper talk (er, yell) for you, it's important to find that filter now so that you can prevent those foot-in-mouth moments from happening later.

Check your sensitivity

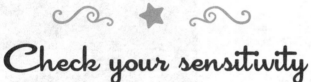

SO HERE'S THE SITCH: You've decided to tell your bud that her breath reeks worse than a cow pasture. So being the blunt babe that you are, you say, "You have seriously bad breath, and guys are gonna gross out if they get within ten feet of you." *Wise move? Um, not quite.* Friends need to be honest, not cruel. So, play it smooth.

The major rule of shooting it straight is to be sensitive: Combat your bud's bad breath—and communicate your point—by buying two tins of mints, one for you and one for her. Pop one and say, "Some cute boys are at the mall—we don't want those onion rings we ate for lunch to linger." *No doubt, she'll follow your lead.* Repeat the mint trick, daily, until it's a habit.

And remember, you don't always have to be so blunt. Sure, your sister's habit of singing in the shower drives you up a (bathroom) wall. But hey, it makes her happy. So before you blast her for less-than-splendid singing skills, simply ask her to turn it down a notch. That way she can still sing—and you can stay sane.

Keep those secrets

And we probably don't need to tell you this, but it's worth a reminder:  Never, ever spill people's secrets. If your BFF's got something juicy all bottled up, and she's dying to tell you, reassure her that you're all ears—and zipped lips. Let her know you're there to listen and that you'd never, ever spill her juice. Then, don't tell anyone. Not a soul. Your bud will return the favor next time you have a secret to share. Swear.

"I accidentally told my BFF about her family's plans to throw her a big surprise birthday party. She says she'll get over it, but I know she's pretty upset. How can I make it up to her?"

GL SAYS . . .

Since you can't undo a mistake (as much as you'd love to press REWIND), it's time to apologize. And don't just say it—show it. Offer up a gesture that genuinely demonstrates your regret. This is your shot at making amends. Nothing says "sorry" like a little extra effort. What to do? Be creative! Give your friend a "month of birthdays" by doing something special for her every Saturday for four weeks. Or plan another surprise party for her in a few months—when she's least expecting it. Granted, this won't erase your gaffe, but it may pave the way for forgiveness.

ANGER MANAGEMENT

Your BFF is late for the movies and you practically bite her head off in the lobby. Sound familiar? Well guess what, girl? Everyone gets angry every once and in a while. Some people react by keeping it bottled up, some yell, some hit things, or slam doors. Some take it out on little siblings or friends. Anger's totally normal . . . until it gets too out-of-control. But, you can learn how to get a handle on this sitch.

Let it all out

Go to your bedroom, grab a pillow, and yell into it as loud as you can. And if you cry, too, hey, you get bonus points. By screaming and yelling, you give your anger a voice and put that energy outside of you where it belongs. *Sometimes you may even want to punch somebody,* so use your pillow if you need to since it's readily available and won't get hurt.

The write stuff

Take all that pent-up anger and spell it out in a diary, journal, or even a letter addressed to *the one who is causing you fury.* Include every fightin' word—totally uncensored. This'll give validity to your thoughts and feelings, and you can also look at it later and see if you want to handle things the same way next time. Can't find the words? There's plenty to be said for scribbling.

Get to talkin'

Sometimes when you're angry, it feels like you've been invaded by a body snatcher who has sucked every ounce of rational thought right out of you. *Cool down by chatting it out with your mom, a friend, or a teacher* to get feedback and, of course, some much-needed sympathy. Talking with someone outside of the situation not only gives you another viewpoint, it can be calming just to have someone really hear you.

Breathe in, breathe out

Your 'rents suddenly retract their OK to let you go to the concert with your crew? Before you spaz, **take a deep breath and count to ten** in your head with your eyes closed. This will get you settled back into a semi-calm state so that you don't blow up.

Figure your triggers

Whether it's getting made fun of, a bad grade, or a particular person, some stuff just makes us angrier than usual. *Learning what makes you mad will help you control your emotions.* If you get mad at your little brother for playing video games, stay away from him while he's doing that!

✦ Solve the problem

If you can resolve the sitches that make you freak out, then there won't be any reason to blow up. Let's say you get mad because your sister hogs the TV. *Come to an agreement* that she can watch when her fave show comes on between 5 and 7 P.M. Then, after that, you get the remote from 7 to 9 o'clock. Problem solved! No more fighting.

✦ Do your body good

Sometimes if you treat your body poorly you're more likely to have mood swings. *Regular exercise can help keep the anger away* since it releases your endorphins (that's feel-good-stuff, FYI!). Eating right can keep you happy and healthy as well, which will give you less severe blow-ups.

Remember, anger is normal, but you need to learn how to control it. By relaxing and thinking about things that make you happy while you feel a freak-out coming on, you can learn to control it and maintain your cool.

THE BOTTOM LINE . . .

You may mess up once in a while, but so what? Your flaws—whether related to your body or your personality—are what makes you, well, you. That's not to say that you shouldn't try to tweak those areas in your life that need improvement. But there's no need to ride the shame train over every gaffe. At some point, you have to move on. File snafus away in your memory so you can take steps not to repeat 'em. It also helps to keep your sense of humor about it all. Looking back, something like calling a guy by the wrong name on a first date could be one of your funniest stories. Mistakes rarely mean your world is ending—just do your very best, then don't sweat the rest.

Tackling the Tough Stuff

6

When you were a little kid, you were probably blissfully unaware of all of the challenging aspects of life. Sadness, anger, scary things like death and divorce likely didn't affect ya all that much. But now that you're older, you're probably more conscious of the hard times—and these emotional ups and downs can make your life feel like a *wild rollercoaster.*

The good news? *Everyone goes though rough patches here and there.* Yep, even the luckiest, most popular, most upbeat people in the world will have some times in their lives when the *bad outweighs the good.* And, sooner or later, all of us need advice to help us feel in control of life's tough situations. That's why we're here. We've been through it all before and are ready to *help you figure out what to do* when you're grieving over Grandma or just battling the blues. You *will* be happier soon—and here's help to *get ya smiling again.*

Dealing With Death

It's inevitable. At some point in our lives, we are all going to have to deal with losing someone. This is one of life's toughest blows. Whether it's a pet, family friend, or grandparent who dies, some mighty powerful feelings get triggered. Meanwhile, everyday life turns upside down—the phone rings off the hook, a major school project is pushed aside, plans are canceled. We're suddenly left to figure out how to say good-bye to the person who died all while comforting others. *We can't provide a magic formula for grieving,* but we can assure you that the severity of pain does ease up and you will find yourself in normal everyday life again. While you're grieving, however, we can offer some help on getting yourself or a friend through the process.

WHAT TO EXPECT

No two people grieve the same way. Psychologists believe there are some likely reactions, but not everybody experiences each of them—and certainly not in any specific order. If your cat is hit by a reckless driver, your initial feeling might be sadness. Or you may be furious. To help you sort through it all, **here are the common reactions** to losing a loved one.

✦ **Disbelief:** Sure, you know the person (or pet) isn't going to walk through the door ever again. Yet, your first thought after news of a death might be, *I can't believe it.* **It's unreal, unimaginable.** It's almost easy sometimes to pretend like it never happened—that's called *denial*. Seems like a good escape, but denying yourself the chance to grieve is actually very harmful to your mental health.

Anger: Death often seems unfair. Even when we know deep down no one is at fault, it feels better to blame someone. Doctors, nurses, pesky sibs, or divine beings make great targets when there's nobody else to resent. **You might even get angry at the deceased person for leaving.** Anyone who's still enjoying the same kind of relationship you lost can become the object of your rage.

Bargaining: When people we care about are injured or ill, we'd do anything to make them recover. Since there usually isn't much we can do, **we fool ourselves into thinking we can bargain for that person's survival.** Even if you're not religious, you might beg a higher power to strike a deal with you.

Loneliness: Ever since the death occurred, you may have had trouble shaking a worried mood or getting the person's image out of your mind. Looming thoughts and feelings can make us feel **removed from reality**, as if we're there but not quite. Believing that others can't possibly comprehend what we're going through can make us feel really lonely.

Feelings of craziness: Being preoccupied also makes us forget things. You're so busy concentrating on the big issues that everyday stuff seems to evaporate from your mind. Forgotten locker combinations, missed book reports, and canceled dates with friends are common. **Some girls may even imagine things.** Emotions that change as often as the weather can also make you feel like you're going crazy. One minute you're crying, the next you're laughing. These experiences are not only normal, but, thankfully, temporary.

Sadness and depression: It's practically impossible not to think about people or pets we loved without becoming sad that they're gone. **Depression can prevent us from enjoying usual activities.** Almost all of the time, bouts with depression don't last too long. But if you're still feeling very sad after a few weeks, then you should seek some outside help (see our section on depression a little later on in this chapter for more info on that).

Guilt and regrets: It's easy to slip into such thoughts as, *I wish I had spent more time with her and told her how much I loved her.* But torturing yourself with what-

ifs and should-haves isn't worthwhile. **Chances are, you did the best you could to show you cared.** But even if you said you hated the person or wished he'd disappear, you did not cause the death! What is said in a moment of anger does not magically occur.

Questioning: Some
people deal with death by trying to make sense of it. Girls ask, "Why did this have to happen to such a good person?" or "What is the meaning behind his death?" **If this is your way, you're not alone.** You could seek out a counselor to help you sort through your beliefs. But you should know that few people ever find definite answers to such colossal questions.

Acceptance: It may seem impossible, but your
feelings—whatever they are—will gradually subside, becoming less sharp. At various times, especially birthdays, anniversaries, and holidays, the pain may come back. But, in general, **you'll realize life must go on** without the person who died. Your world won't ever be the same, but the person or pet will live on through your memories.

Coping With It ALL

All of these emotions are undoubtedly new and confusing to you. And it can be hard to know how to deal when you're feeling so down. But please know that you can get support and that things will get better in time, especially when you're armed with some key coping skills.

PUT IT OUT THERE, IN PRIVATE

We know it's not gonna be easy, but you need to get your feelings out so you don't bottle it all up inside. Even if it's not talking to anyone about it just yet, try jotting your thoughts down in a journal. It's a lot more helpful than you might think. Write down some of your favorite memories you had with your lost loved one. You could even pen her a letter telling her how you feel or what you'd really like to tell her.

SHARE YOUR FEELINGS

Most likely, you're not the only one feeling the way you do right now. Your other friends and family are probably experiencing the same sort of thing, and it could be helpful if you all sat down and talked about it.

● ● ● ● ● ● ● ● ● ●

Express yourself better with writing? Type out a speech or obituary. You might feel tons better if you write a story about what the person meant to you. Read it at the funeral or family gathering, or have someone else read it for you. Whatever you do, it'll be comforting to know you're not alone.

GET A KEEPSAKE

Memories comfort. *They allow us to keep people alive in our minds.* Keepsakes we can look at and touch help maintain vivid memories. If you can, ask to have something that belonged to your loved one. Photos, clothes, or whimsical items (Grandma's egg timer, a baseball cap, a coffee mug) make great physical reminders.

● ● ● ● ● ● ● ● ● ● ● ●

MAKE A SCRAPBOOK

Collect pictures and mementos from the occasions you shared with the pet or person who died and *paste them into a scrapbook.* Write captions or stories to remember the good times you had together.

● ● ● ● ● ● ● ● ● ● ● ●

GET HELP GETTING HELP

Another way to get help? *Turn to your parents.* They love you and want you to be happy and healthy. If you want to start seeing a counselor, ask them for advice. Even if your school doesn't have one, search your local place of worship for someone to talk to or even a support group.

HELP!

"My friend's grandmother recently passed away and she is so sad. What can I do to help her cope?"

Thinking of You

GL SAYS...

There's no perfect phrase to recite when someone is grieving. But even small gestures make the people you care about—and you—feel way better. It's OK to tell the person, "I'm sorry to hear your relative died. Are you OK?" Many girls wonder if they'll cause more hurt if they speak of the deceased. Usually the opposite is true. Most mourners feel better talking about their loved ones. Just listening is probably the most comforting thing you can do.

Parental PROBS

You may not have experienced a mega loss yet. But sometimes, problems between your parents—especially separation and divorce—can feel like a death, too. The prospect of your parents splitting up can be pretty harsh—as is listening to the 'rents fight every night. But as much as your parents argue, you've gotta know it's not your fault. If Mom and Dad are getting divorced, it's because of each other, not you. They may have a lot of differences, but they do have one thing in common: their brilliant, beautiful daughter (that's you!). So here's how to keep from getting caught in the middle of Mom and Dad—and your sanity.

The best of both worlds

Just 'cause you're the middleman doesn't mean you have to pick a side. They're your parents, so how in the world are you supposed to choose? And really, they shouldn't expect you to! That just adds a ton of pressure that is so unnecessary. If they disagree, that's one thing. But it's neither fair nor right for them to drag you into it.

Now talk it out

Feeling the weighty pressure of holding your parents' relationship together can affect your health and well-being. You might even experience stress-related symptoms, such as headaches, stomachaches, sleeplessness, or anxiety. If you're bogged down by your parents' marital problems,

118

tell them. If they try to skate around the issue, stand firm: You might say, "I feel nervous when you ask me to be the go-between," or, "It makes me sad when you say bad things about each other. Can you, please, leave me out of it from now on?" *Don't back down—you need to take care of you.*

🌀 Give it time

Eventually, life will settle down for ya and your family. It just might not happen as fast as you want it to. If they continue to maintain this messy triangle, try to get a trusted teacher, guidance counselor, or relative to intervene on your behalf. *On the meantime, keep yourself busy* with the stuff kids are supposed to be occupied with—like having fun.

Other Troubles At Home

Between social tangles, endless tests and quizzes, and too-frequent tiffs with sibs, you probably have more than enough, thankyouverymuch, on your emotional plate. The last thing—wait, make that the *very* last thing—you need is more stress.

It really stinks when, to top it all off, someone in the fam is going through a tough time. You might not even be sure what's brewing. But something's up. You don't need to be Nancy Drew to detect the looks, long silences, raised voices, painful vibes, even tear-reddened eyes. Constant what-ifs ("What if this happens?") torture you day and night. One thing you know for sure—there's a Big Problem.

Major dilemmas usually bring on intense, yucky feelings that are often hard to deal with. What to say? What not to say? What to do to help? Chances are you've never been in this kind of predicament before. Although there are few "rights" and "wrongs," we can offer you ways to get through this tough family time.

● ● ● ● ● ●

Get the scoop

Many girls say the worst is not knowing what has the 'rents in an uproar. When you don't know what's going on, your imagination can go crazy—along with your panic. Don't be shy about asking Mom or Dad to clarify the situation. Find a quiet time to say, "You seem upset. What's the problem?

Please share it with me." Sometimes, parents prefer to keep things **under wraps** to prevent you from being burdened with adult problems or because it's a private issue.

But you can always explain to your parents that not knowing is scary. Without nosing around for details, say, "I don't need specifics, but please tell me if my worst fears are true. Is someone sick? Is Dad going to lose his job?" This straightforward approach might banish your most horrendous thoughts.

● ● ● ● ● ●

Don't forget about Y-O-U

Parental problems can spark a multitude of messed-up stuff. First off, stressed 'rents are often less available for you—that school project you need help with, or the ride you and your buds desperately need to the movies on Friday night. *Many girls feel rotten about these "selfish" feelings.* The thinking goes, *My parents are trying their best, so I shouldn't complain.*

Sure, it would be terrific if you could offer 100-percent support 24/7/365, but you're human. It's perfectly OK to want your life **back to normal.** Your needs can be shoved aside during a crisis, and it's hard. Particularly when you have added chores or responsibilities, or when your parents depend on you to comfort them, you might think, *Hey, wait; I'm the kid around here!*

Don't be ashamed

Being embarrassed about your family situation adds additional stress. Let's say your brother just got busted for drugs and is going to be shipped off to military school. You may think this is way too shameful to share with your friends, but **keeping your feelings inside is unhealthy.** Remember that yours is neither the first nor the only family to have problems. Nobody's family is perfect.

If, however, you get specific instructions from the 'rents that the problem is classified and you can't spill, try vaguely telling friends or teachers, "I'm having a tough time right now because of a family problem." If they still pry, say, "I'm not comfortable getting specific," "It's personal," or "I'm not allowed to talk about it, but thanks for your concern." Easy as that.

● ● ● ● ● ●

Stay positive

Despite your best efforts, there's little chance you can fix the problem or take away your parents' hurt. If you're unsure what to do, ask directly, "How can I help?" Maybe you can't cure your grandmother's illness, or get your dad to move back home. But during nerve-racking times, your parents would surely appreciate you getting up for school without seven reminders, an unloaded dishwasher, or a squabble-free dinner hour. *It's also important to stay positive* and do things that make you feel better: throw a fun sleepover, get out of the house for a run, or just window shop at the mall . . . anything to get your mind off the tension at home.

SERIOUSLY SAD

With all of the emotional ups and downs in your life, it can be hard to separate temporary sadness from the more serious signs of depression. Stressful sitches (like the loss of a loved one, probs at home, or even bad grades) can instantly make it feel like the entire world's against ya.

But when the sadness ceases to stop after two weeks, and you've got minimal motivation to get out of bed, go to school, or hang out with your friends or family, then you may be battling something much bigger than the blues. It could be depression. But how do you know when you (or a bud) is not just having a big bummer of the week—but honestly depressed? Here's a few answers to your questions to clear up the confusion.

123

"When I'm feeling lousy and crying for no reason at all, how can I tell if it's because of depression or just PMS?"

Hey, hormones are chemicals. And during puberty, *your body's hormones are constantly, increasing, decreasing, or just plain doing whatever they feel like.* But all of this affects your emotions. Each month, before you get your period, the number of hormones in your body increases, causing you to be more emotional than usual. But even when you're not having your period, those chemicals are still doing the mambo. Given all the changes that are going on, it's no wonder girls feel moody, irritable, and lonely. One minute you're sobbing enough to fill your sister's kiddie pool and laughing like a hyena the next. *This isn't depression—it's normal.*

"I only get bummed on weekends, when I should be having fun. What's wrong with me?"

Take solace in knowing that it is not at all uncommon for teens to feel crummy on Sundays. Why? Think about how you usually feel on Fridays. The weekend is coming . . . no school, fun stuff to do, and you can sleep in! You're psyched, right? Some people see Sundays in just the opposite way. *Sundays marks the end of the weekend—the party's over.* Ugh.

You can also get bummed around the end of summer vacay or the end of a holiday. While people like to joke about school being a drag, it helps your mood to change your overall outlook on your week. *Don't just live for the weekends.* Start looking forward to the special things that each day brings—even if it's just a compliment from the tennis coach on your serve or tater tots at lunch.

The seasons and the weather also contribute to your mood. When it's late fall, for instance, the sky is gray and everything looks dead. You've got to stay inside, so that means you can't even enjoy what little sunlight there is. Near the center of the brain is a gland that is affected by light. Researchers believe that significant decreases in sunlight can lead you to feel down and dreary, just like the weather! *Make it a point to walk outside* and soak up what little sun there is.

● ● ● ● ● ●

"What is the deal with depression? Does being stressed mean I'm depressed?"

Depression can happen to the most popular girl in school. Some depressed girls appear smart, pretty, and confident on the surface, only dealing with their real feelings once they are alone. Depression isn't picky. *Anyone can become depressed*—millions of teens

125

suffer from this condition. It's also possible that just like you inherited your dad's dimples, you may have a gene that makes you more depression-prone.

If you think you're depressed, confide in a trusted adult before you continue your downward spiral. It's best if you can tell one of your parents, but if you can't, it's important to talk to a school counselor, a relative, a close friend of the family, or your doctor. *Tell them how you are feeling and what is upsetting you.* Do not try to be strong, just be honest

with how you feel. If you have thoughts about hurting yourself in any way, it's important that you tell them that, too. *Don't hesitate. Just do it.*

THE BOTTOM LINE . . .

Sad stuff is inevitable. And whether your grandma was just diagnosed with cancer or your pet pooch passed, just know that this intense heartache will eventually heal. No matter how devastated you may be now. And the crazy thing is, enduring the tough stuff will help ya learn tons about yourself—like how to deal with your feelings, how to let people comfort you, and how to care for other people going through a similar sitch. So keep your head up! You *can* cope—and come out a stronger sistah as a result.

Index

The advice girls are looking for about practically everything!

From breakouts to periods, eating right and everything in between, this guide delivers the body basics to help you look and feel fabulous!

Learn to get through tough times and max out on your best moments with advice on how to handle first day jitters, fights with friends, and more!

You can't avoid all drama, but this guide will help you keep it together and learn how to deal with guys, friends, family, and more!

Should I take French or Spanish? Get the skills you need to make decisions stress free!

SCHOLASTIC

www.scholastic.com/girlslife

GLF10